THE STRUM BOWING METHOD

HOW TO GROOVE ON STRINGS

By Tracy Silverman
Foreword by Darol Anger

Edited by Julie Lyonn Lieberman and Louisa Silverman
Layout by Austin Gray   www.entireworld.us
Painting by Rachel Kice   wwww.rachelkice.com

Copyright © 2018 by Tracy Silverman
All rights reserved.

No part of this book may be reproduced or transmitted in any form or by any means, electronic or mechanical, including photocopying, recording, or by any information storage and retrieval systems without written permission from the author or publisher, except for the inclusion of brief quotations in a review.

Published by Silverman Musical Enterprises, LLC
Nashville, TN
info@tracysilverman.com | www.tracysilverman.com | www.strumbowing.com

Dedication

This book is dedicated to the next generation of string players and teachers, whose innovations will hopefully soon make this book obsolete.

Strum Bowing \ˈstrəm ˈbō-iŋ\ *noun*
Using a bow like you're strumming a guitar.

The Strum Bowing Method presents a clear and comprehensive approach for string players to easily learn how to play and teach the grooves in contemporary popular music.

Popular music relies heavily on a strong underlying rhythm, or "groove." Contemporary grooves are foundational to the study of guitar, drums and other instruments, and they are essential to playing in jazz and rock ensembles. String playing, however, comes largely from the classical tradition grounded in 18th and 19th century European music. The result is that young string players are not being taught how to play the music of their own contemporary musical culture. **The time has come to retool our playing—for ourselves, for our students, and for the greater groove!**

A Simple, Unified Approach

This area of post-classical string playing is so new that a comprehensive pedagogy hasn't yet been developed, and there is a palpable need for a simple, unified approach. Strum Bowing encompasses all the different alternative bow techniques—Chops, Shuffles, Ghost Notes, etc.—by targeting the common thread linking grooves in all styles: the subdivision of the beat.

The best entry point to contemporary popular styles is through rhythm, and for string players, the way to the rhythm is through the bow. With Strum Bowing, you **physicalize the subdivision** with your bow as if you were strumming a guitar, creating grooves by bringing out accents and dropping Ghost Notes.

In this book, we will approach Strum Bowing as:
- **Horizontal**—often known by fiddlers as a *shuffle*
- **Vertical**—known to many as the *Chop*
- **3D Strum**—the combination of horizontal and vertical bowing techniques for playing chords, melodies and/or bass lines

We'll learn how to use grooves as the entry point to improvisation as well as how to bring rhythmic vitality to classical music.

The Strum Bowing Method functions as both a how-to manual for the amateur or professional player and as the conductor/instructor companion to **22 Groove Studies for Strings,** a collection of Strum Bowing etudes for middle school through college level string ensembles.

The Strum Bowing Method is effective with students of all ages because it's so easy to learn. **Strum Bowing doesn't focus on the complexity of rhythm; it focuses on the simplicity.**

Just strum.

Praise for *The Strum Bowing Method*

"My old partner in the Turtle Island String Quartet, the brilliant violinist Tracy Silverman, has distilled the essence of what we did with string rhythms down to a pretty exact science, and does it with humor and warmth. I don't know how someone could go through this book and not come out grooving!"

Darol Anger
Founding member, Turtle Island String Quartet
Associate Professor, Berklee College of Music
www.darolanger.com

"Tracy has done it! This is what string players have been waiting for—rhythm and groove playing are the last frontier of our string world. Finally, the master electric violin player is leading you to the promised land. Tracy's book will ignite the 'turbow' in your music!"

Mark Wood
7-String Electric Violinist, founder of Wood Violins,
Mark Wood Rock Orchestra Camp, Electrify Your Strings
www.markwoodmusic.com

"At last! Tracy Silverman has developed an indispensable curriculum for string players and teachers. This is the missing link in string education: the heart and art of the Groove. I guarantee his approach will enable you to play ANY style better, particularly the styles string pedagogy has ignored."

Julie Lyonn Lieberman
Eclectic Styles Maven, Author, Educator
www.julielyonn.com

"With *The Strum Bowing Method*, Tracy Silverman presents a "grand unified theory" of how to groove with visceral authenticity. Simple, yet profound, Tracy's approach achieves immediate and far-reaching results for string players ranging from beginners to seasoned professionals. Whether you're seeking to play contemporary styles like rock, jazz, and hip hop, or simply looking to play Mozart or fiddle music with maximum rhythmic drive, this method is for you!"

David "Doc" Wallace
Chair of the String Dept., Berklee College of Music
www.docwallacemusic.com

"*The Strum Bowing Method*" is a must-have for any string player who wants to participate in dance-based music. Tracy Silverman has created the go-to method book that makes groove accessible. He starts from the vantage point of rhythm as the driving force of musical expression. Focusing on the groove offers a new and much-needed perspective in string pedagogy. Insightful explanations combined with fun, productive exercises provide an easy entryway for any classically-trained string player. I'm certain that "*The Strum Bowing Method*" will take its place alongside scale studies and etude books as essential for the contemporary string player. It will be required reading for my students."

Mimi Rabson
Associate Professor, Berklee College of Music
www.mimirabson.com

"Tracy has taken on the gargantuan task of producing a book that explains all this rhythm and chopping stuff in extremely detailed but simple, easy-to-understand language. A few years ago I saw a YouTube video he casually produced from his dorm room at a Mark O'Connor fiddle camp wherein he mentioned a concept that actually blew my mind. Even as the inventor of this technique I had never formally realized that all this stuff is ON A GRID!

"*The Strum Bowing Method* is absolutely brilliant. I have absolute confidence that if this user's manual on playing rhythm violin is studied carefully and completely by any string player, the student *will groove*."

Richard Greene
Violinist, legendary "Inventor of the Chop"
www.richardgreene.net

"Tracy Silverman is one of the most invested, precise, and imaginative musicians I have ever met and played with. His Strum Bowing reveals all the technical mysteries involved in string players creating groove-based music. Systematically, Tracy shows you how to unlock the boundless artistry of groove-based playing locked within more traditional methods. This book is the key towards a new relationship to your instrument, your music-making, and your ability to create new worlds of sound, every time your play."

Daniel Bernard Roumain (DBR)
Professor of Practice & Institute Professor
Herberger Institute for Design and the Arts (ASU)
www.danielroumain.com

"Exploring a realm of instruction most often reserved for drummers and percussionists, Tracy Silverman has concocted a singular and definitive manual of extended rhythmic technique for the violin and presented a breathtakingly broad rhythmic discussion that has never existed for string players. Even if a student has no connection to groove-based music and popular forms or jazz, working through this book will enhance musicianship and improve the fundamental feel of their playing - from Bach to Bartok. Tracy reminds us that ALL music has a groove, and can be studied in that context. *The Strum Bowing Method* is as complete a statement on the subject as it's possible to make."

Danny Seidenberg
Violist (Turtle Island String Quartet)
www.dannyseidenberg.com

"Tracy's brilliant performance abilities and groundbreaking educational approach have been huge influences on the growing community of rhythmic string players. This book will undoubtedly go down in history as a definitive treatise on the subject. Much gratitude for the time and thought that Tracy has put into this project. We couldn't ask for a better guru!"

Mike Block
Cello (Silk Road Ensemble)
Associate Professor, Berklee College of Music
www.mikeblockmusic.com

"Tracy Silverman continues to break ground with this great resource"

Chris Howes
Jazz Violinist, Educator
www.christianhowes.com

"One of the world's most innovative electric violinists covers a topic that has rarely been addressed in string education. This book is a must read for all string players who want to get their groove on! It's about time someone wrote a book on grooving, a skill so vital for every string player, and who better to do it than one of the hardest grooving pioneers of the electric violin, Tracy Silverman!"

Joe Deninzon
Rock Violinist (Stratospheerius)
www.joedeninzon.com

"A book so good it could ruin my career."

Alex DePue
Violinist (Steve Vai)
www.alexdepue.com

"Tracy Silverman's *The Strum Bowing Method* is a monumental step in filling a huge gap in modern string pedagogy and will be a powerful force in promoting the American Music System's "3M principle" – Music is More than Melody. This comprehensive system of training the fundamental rhythmic component of American music styles will greatly further the mission of holistic music education in America and beyond."

Pam Wiley
President, American Music System
www.americanmusicsystem.com

"This is the comprehensive, go-to guide for rhythmic playing on the violin. I wish I had had access to this when I was a high school student. I would have avoided many years of mistakes and sub-par playing. This book is a necessary and vital tool for the modern string player who wishes to transcend stifling traditions, destroy the old boundaries of string playing, and walk his or her own path."

Earl Maneein
Violin, (SEVEN)SUNS, Black Heart Sutra
www.earlmaneeinmusic.com

"Tracy's book on his concept of *The Strum Bowing Method* is a thoroughgoing approach to deepen perception and skill at using the bow in a rhythmically articulate fashion. As the wand is to a wizard, the bow is to a fiddler! This book is magical."

Billy Contreras
Jazz Violinist
String Department, Belmont University
www.belmont.edu/music/faculty/faculty_listing_a-g/Contreras_Billy.html

Meeting Tracy Silverman nearly 20 years ago was a humbling and eye-opening experience - there are incredible things that can be done on the violin that go well beyond virtuoso classical technique. With the release of "Strum Bowing," Tracy's amazing innovations are ready to take over and transform the world; the non-grooving string player will soon be as obsolete at the rotary phone.

Rachel Barton Pine
Concert Violinist, Recording Artist
www.rachelbartonpine.com

"Bowed strings combine basic chording with a range of expression and vocal-like lyricism that has forever been the envy of players of every other type of instrument. The closest things we have to weaknesses are clarity and strength of signal for amping and processing, and a ready ability to contribute to the rhythmic bed. Modern pickup tech and instrument design is fixing the first problem; Tracy Silverman just fixed the second."

Chuck Bontrager (Tributosaurus)
Concertmaster, Hamilton Chicago Orchestra
www.chuckbontrager.com

"It's here at last! I can't wait to use this book to help my students learn chopping and rhythm techniques….this is going to make it so easy! One of the things I love most about this book is how much Tracy's personality and humor shine through. It's obvious that he loves to groove and wants to share and spread the love. Congrats, my friend!"

Tammy Rogers-King
Violinist (The Steel Drivers)
String Department, Belmont University
www.tammyrogers.com

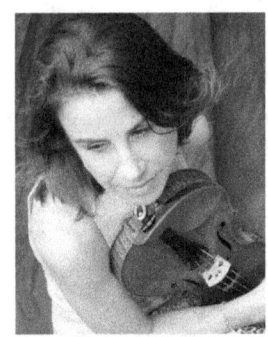

"*The Strum Bowing Method* is a brilliant, ground-breaking pedagogical treatise that takes its place at the heart of universal musical language. *The Strum Bowing Method* focuses on unlocking our rhythmic inner-self and offers clarity for string players and teachers who wish to adventure beyond the boundaries of the codified Classical vernacular."

Elisabeth Small
Chair of the String Department, Belmont University
www.elisabethsmall.com

"Tracy's book focuses on the simplicity of the rhythm, rather than the complexity. I look forward to teaching using this book and look forward to a time when as a composer and arranger, we count on strings as the go-to section for the groove. Dance, sing and groovon."

Bert Ligon
Professor of Jazz / Director of Jazz Studies, University of South Carolina
www.sc.edu/study/colleges_schools/music/faculty-staff/Ligon.php

"These are exciting times to be alive in a string player's body. Beginning with the advent of the Chop in the 1960's and now with the addition of Tracy's Strum Bowing technique, new realms of music and uncharted territories of creation are opening for those who wield a bow. Look out electric guitar, here we come."

Casey Driessen
Program Director, Master of Music in Contemporary Performance, Berklee College of Music, Valencia
www.caseydriessen.com

"Tracy has written what will likely go down as the seminal strum bowing history hall of fame explanation of the entire strum bowing art form. Students of eclectic string playing will likely gravitate to this thorough and expertly written manual as the perfect way to explain the seemingly unexplainable and explore the somewhat uncharted territory of rhythmic bow style. Written in an easy-to-follow manner and sequenced so that even a novice player will be able to correctly explore the strum bow style, this brainchild of Tracy's incredible right arm and bow hand will profoundly influence generations of adventurous string players of all genres!"

Daryl Silberman
Orchestra director, Waubonsie Valley High School, clinician, performer
www.daryls.com

"Strum Bowing is a tremendous new resource for string players. The development of high level right-hand rhythm skills are essential tools in the arsenal of any contemporary string player. This book becomes the essential 'road map' for chopping and beyond. The pedagogy is logical, progressive, and easy to understand. I highly recommend this bold new addition to the canon of string pedagogy."

Bob Phillips
Director of String Publications, Alfred Music
www.phillipsfiddlers.com

"When I heard Tracy was going to write about his strum bowing I was immediately interested because the rhythm of the bow has been an integral part of my musical journey. Getting another perspective in this neglected area is a very valuable thing, especially when it comes from someone like Tracy who has carved out such a unique approach to the fiddle."

Martin Hayes
Irish fiddler (The Gloaming, The Martin Hayes Quartet)
www.martinhayes.com

Table of Contents

Foreword by Darol Anger — xii

Preface — xiv
    About Notation — xix
    About Repeats — xx
    About the Video Demonstrations — xx
    About *22 Groove Studies for Strings* — xx

Acknowledgements — xxii

Part I: The Strum—The Heart of the Groove — 1

Introduction to Strum Bowing — 2

1. The Groovon: The Smallest Particle of the Groove — 10
    Thriving in the Rhythm Section—Mimi Rabson — 18

2. The Grid: The Structure of Grooves — 20
    The Future of Strings in the 21st Century—Mark Wood — 26

3. Strum 101: Getting your Groovon — 28

4. Ghost Notes: How to *Not* Play an Instrument — 32
    Strum Bowing and the Modern Bow—David "Doc" Wallace — 38

5. Placekeeper Notes: Locking to the Grid — 40
    The Lyrical, Rhythmical Life of the Irish Bow—Martin Hayes — 48

6. If You Can Say It, You Can Play It: The Power of Vocalizing — 50
    Thinking as a (Black) Violinist—Daniel Bernard Roumain — 54

7. The Dance of the Groove: The Power of Physicalizing — 56
    Bow Circles—Darol Anger — 60

8. GPS: Groove Proficiency System, Practice Groove 1 — 62

9. GPS: Groove Proficiency System, Practice Groove 2 — 70
    Finding the Funk—Joe Deninzon — 74

10. GPS: Groove Proficiency System, Practice Groove 3 — 76

11. Variety is the Spice of Grooves: The Power of the Strum — 86

    Brütal Bow Technique 101—Earl Maneein — 92

12. Triplets and other Odd-ities: Alternating Accents — 94

Part II: The Vertical Strum—The Chop and Beyond — 107

13. Going Vertical—Part 1: The Chop — 108

    The Chop: Relaxing the Right Hand—Richard Greene — 114

14. Going Vertical—Part 2: The Compound Chop — 116

    Chopping on Cello vs Violin—Mike Block — 120

15. Groovin' the Chop: Vertical Grooves — 122

    String Drumming—Julie Lyonn Lieberman — 128

16. The 3-D Strum—Part 1: Horizontal and Vertical Combined — 130

17. The 3-D Strum—Part 2: 3-D Versions of the Practice Grooves — 132

    The Vertical Vector—Pam Wiley — 136

18. The 3-D Strum—Part 3: Chords and Harmony — 138

19. Rhythmic Improvisation: Strumming Solos — 146

    All Notes Are Not Created Equal—Rachel Barton Pine — 136

20. The Rhythm of Melody: Bringing Strum Bowing Into Classical Playing — 152

Glossary — 166

Foreword

THE DAY I MET TRACY SILVERMAN was the day he auditioned for the first chair slot in the Turtle Island String Quartet. One of our founding members, David Balakrishnan, had to leave, and we were pretty worried about whether we would be able to maintain the character and technical level of the group. I remember being concerned with Tracy's relaxed manner on the phone, wondering if we were just going to have to keep looking for what seemed impossible back then: a young violinist who could sight-read, improvise in lots of different contemporary styles, and have cool hair.

What happened then was that Tracy came in, made everyone feel relaxed, and sight-read on the spot all the TISQ's complicated charts. He also played a bunch of interesting solos on the tunes in various styles, and he played with a solid groove. He approached playing on the highest string of his violin as if it were the lowest string—I don't know another way of describing it except to say that he sounded like he was carving tone right out of his violin.

To say I was impressed would be an understatement, but he was so easy about fitting in with the group's sound and direction that we immediately hit it off. He was interested in my explorations into all the "Chopping" rhythm techniques and had worked out slightly different but parallel solutions to the challenge of getting the violin to groove within the rhythm. His casual approach to violin playing grew out of a solid and sure technique that enabled him to do pretty much anything on the violin, accompanied by a charming lack of pretension and judgment about any of it. I remember thinking: "What is this? This guy doesn't even care how good he is...he just enjoys making music! It's just plain fun to play with this guy!"

Tracy's clarity and matter-of-fact attitude about the violin and music in general helped stabilize a lot of my thoughts on these matters, and his imaginative and resourceful compositional mind helped the TISQ grow into rock and Brazilian musical territory and helped us develop a strong point-of-view toward western European art music and jazz. And his cool hair and articulate mastery of many violin techniques really helped too, especially as the group developed a really fun and informative outreach program, in which we helped younger string musicians become aware of the vastly expanding musical choices available to string players from any tradition. We grew to be friends and mutual admirers over the succeeding years, asking and answering many musical questions for and with each other, even after we both moved on from the TISQ. It's always a cool surprise to check in with Tracy and find out what rich or radical music project he is pursuing, whether using intricate electronics and recording devices to augment his sound, designing new violin-type instruments to play, or collaborating with some of the giants of contemporary music in any style or field. And he does it all with good humor, creativity, and a no-nonsense attitude that is still refreshing—not to mention a great groove. And to hear him explain all this as he invents it is a pleasure.

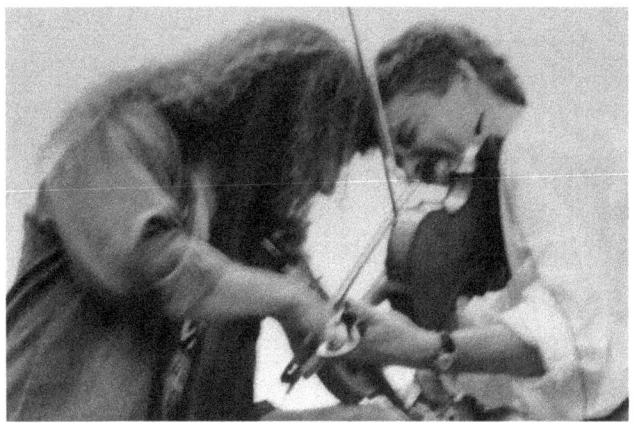

That's why I'm really happy that the string world will now have this great, swingin' resource that clearly explains so much of what we—and so many other musicians—obsess over every day: the groove.

Darol Anger
Spring 2018

Preface

Why Strum Bowing?

There has been a quiet revolution going on in the string-playing world. Once again, string players are finding an authentic voice in the popular music of their time.

In many ways, this revolution marks a return to the past. All the masterpieces of the classical repertoire were written in the popular idiom of each composer's time and place. Mozart wrote in the fashionable Viennese style of the late 1700's, Verdi's melodies became the pop songs of his day, sung all over Italy in the mid 1800's and Tschaikovsky composed in the Russian style that was taking Europe by storm in the late 1800's.

But somewhere in the mid-20th century, classical music and popular music started to become two different things. Composers of serious concert music, feeling that the harmonic language of tonality had been fully explored, moved forward into atonal music—music without a tonal center.

String playing became frozen in time and remained more or less in a state of arrested development.

Meanwhile, popular music continued to develop and flourish, as it always does, in the vernacular idiom of its time and place, giving birth to blues, jazz, rock and all the popular music of the 20th century.

The general audience, alienated by the inaccessibility of atonality, gravitated either toward more accessible popular music or backward to the more familiar masterpieces of the past. And string playing, as taught in conservatories all around the world, became frozen in time and remained more or less in a state of arrested development with an overwhelming emphasis on the European styles of the 18th and 19th centuries.

Strings took a back seat in popular music, and the dominant instruments became saxophone in jazz, guitar in rock and digital instruments in hip-hop, with keyboards finding a role in everything. The rest of the music world continued to evolve in a fairly contemporary landscape, but classical string playing held to the traditions of the past.

Get in the Groove

Tired of sitting on the sidelines, contemporary string players are now striving to find a place for themselves in their own popular musical culture. The new role for strings must include a vernacular melodic voice, one that is closer to a pop vocal style and contemporary melodic instruments like electric guitar and saxophone. It must also include the ability to reflect the rhythmic character of these groove-based styles. The time has come for every string teacher—from elementary schools to conservatories—to teach their students the art of the groove.

That's why I wrote this book.

Young players want to learn pop songs they are familiar with, so middle school and high school string teachers have begun to incorporate more non-classical music in their curricula. Doing so has enabled string programs to compete for the school budget that tends to favor band and chorus over strings. A flood of pop, rock and jazz arrangements have been published to help fill this new need. But the old refrain that "strings can't swing" or "strings don't have good rhythm" hasn't gone away. In fact, playing contemporary pop music just highlights this perception.

Whether it's swing, rock or hip hop, the idea that string players sound square is not going to go away unless they actually learn how to groove.

The time has come for every string teacher—from elementary schools to conservatories—to teach their students the art of the groove.

The idea that string players sound square is not going to go away unless they actually learn how to groove.

But playing with a groove is not something that most string teachers have ever learned how to do, let alone teach. Nobody taught me, and I started playing when I was 5 years old and graduated from the Juilliard School. It took years of playing in rock bands, wedding bands, recording sessions and jam sessions—what I think of as my post-graduate work—for me to discover how much I didn't know.

It's All About the Bow

The result of this new demand for post-classical playing is that there's been a huge thirst for "alternative" or "eclectic" strings resources and pedagogy.

Whether your background is classical or from the fiddle world, conservatory trained or self-taught, this book will help you find your authentic groove by guiding you towards the overarching natural law of every groove-based style of music: the primacy of the subdivision of the beat. And on strings, subdivision is all about the bow.

Especially in classical music, strings are primarily melodic instruments. We're not accustomed to functioning like a rhythm guitar player in the rhythm section. But playing rhythm is fun. It makes people dance. Luckily, the bow is an incredibly versatile tool capable of a limitless world of rhythmic sound.

The Strum Bowing Method will not only help you develop the vertical stroke called "the Chop," it will also open the door to the wide world of rhythm that exists in that vast land between the horizontal *detache* and the vertical Chop, what I call the "3-D Strum."

This book should help any string player easily develop a natural approach to rhythm and grooves, the heart of contemporary pop music.

And it's simpler than you may think.

The Path Less Traveled

I started playing violin when I was very young, and I was lucky enough to study with some of the best classical teachers around, including Morris Gomberg and Debbra Schwartz at the Chicago Musical College, Ivan Galamian, Lewis Kaplan and Sam Rhodes at The Juilliard School, among others. But somewhere along the way at Juilliard I took a left turn. All the music I heard around me outside of school—rock, jazz, film and TV scores, international music—started opening my ears and eyes to a wider world outside of my classical studies. I adored all the great violin concertos and revered the great violin virtuosos, but my friends from high school didn't know about the Sibelius concerto and had never heard of Jascha Heifetz. For them, it was all about guitar heroes: Jimi Hendrix, Eric Clapton, Carlos Santana, Jimmy Page. I wanted to play music that people outside the classical world would like, music that my high school buddies would rock out to, music in my own contemporary American musical language. I started out at The Juilliard School hoping to be the next Jascha Heifetz and left wanting to be the next Jimi Hendrix.

I considered switching to guitar but decided to retool my violin technique instead. After graduating from Juilliard, I made my living for about a dozen years playing everything from strolling violin at the Plaza Hotel to string quartets for wedding ceremonies, from jazz violin at cocktail hours to singing in a wedding band. And all the while, I was leading my own rock bands at clubs like CBGB's and the China Club in New York on electric 6-string violin.

Right out of school, I met another ex-Juilliard player, Mark Wood. He had built the first 6-string violins and shared my conviction that the electric violin was the future. Mark built my first electric instrument, and I was an immediate convert. Over the next thirty-five years, I continued to build and design my own instruments. The dream was to get kids to play air violin instead of air guitar. Mark and I both raced to be the first electric violin rock star. We wanted to prove that the electric

I started out at The Juilliard School hoping to be the next Jascha Heifetz and left wanting to be the next Jimi Hendrix.

> *After about ten years of this, I realized I had stumbled upon some pretty effective and very un-classical ways of using my bow.*

violin could do everything the electric guitar could do. I purposely had no guitar in my rock bands to force myself to learn how to become a rhythm player as well as a lead player. After about ten years, I realized I had stumbled upon some pretty effective and very untraditional ways of using my bow.

After years of grinding it out in the NY, and later Minneapolis, rock scenes, my big break came out of left field when I was asked to join the Turtle Island String Quartet. TISQ violinist, Darol Anger, taught me how to Chop, and my years of touring with Darol, Mark Summer and Danny Seidenberg was a musical education of the very highest level. Since then, my hybrid skill set has opened some unexpected doors leading to the premieres of electric violin concertos written for me by John Adams, Terry Riley, Nico Muhly and Kenji Bunch, solo performances at Carnegie Hall, Disney Hall, Royal Albert Hall and other venues, and three electric violin concertos of my own.

And all along the way I taught violin.

Teaching—The Best Way to Learn

This book is for string teachers as well as string players.

Leonard Bernstein said that teaching is the best way to learn, and I've had the opportunity to learn from a really wide spectrum of student string players. I'm currently on the faculty at Belmont University in Nashville, TN, and I have taught at Vanderbilt University's Blair School of Music, Macalester College, the Mark O'Connor Fiddle Camp, the Mark Wood Rock Orchestra Camp, Stanford Jazz Workshop and Jazz in July at U Mass Amherst. I've also given residencies at Brown and Vanderbilt Universities, and I present frequent clinics and workshops all around the world.

Over the years I have developed techniques for playing and teaching rock, jazz and improvisation to string players of all levels. I've had the opportunity to see what these players really need, what they tend to have trouble with, to bounce my ideas off them and to learn from them what works and what doesn't. This was essential to the process of figuring out how to teach something new to a general audience of string players.

As a player who has made this journey myself, I intimately understand how to make this method effective and easy for the player. I've read books about jazz that seem to glory in obfuscation, needlessly over-complicating things as if to say, "See how smart I am?" With *The Strum Bowing Method* I've taken exactly the opposite approach—I hope to show you how simple it is. My motto is, "If guitar players can do it, how hard could it be?"

It's been gratifying to see the immediate and dramatic results for my students. And it's actually a good thing that I didn't put this book out years ago when I first started writing it because now I've had well over a decade of workshops and private lessons to refine and tweak a rough approach into a very specific sequence of tips, definitions, instructions, examples, nomenclature and notation. I think I've finally figured out how to get this across.

Strum Bowing is much more than just some gimmicky tricks with the bow. My hope is to make it easier for the next generation of string players to fully participate in their own musical culture. My dream is to see high school kids rocking out to their favorite tunes—playing air violin.

If guitar players can do it, how hard could it be?

About Notation

♩ (×) = Ghost Note

♩ (/) = Chop

♩ (/ ghost) = Ghost Chop

♩ (○) = Air Strum

My dream is to see high school kids rocking out to their favorite tunes—playing air violin.

About Repeats

I have used repeat signs in most of the examples throughout the book. These are all intended as open repeats, meaning you should repeat them as many times as needed when practicing, not just once.

About the Video Demonstrations

The camera icon (▶) indicates a streaming video clip demonstrating the example. You will find these clips on StrumBowing.com

About *22 Groove Studies for Strings*

The Strum Bowing Method is intended as both a how-to book for the individual user and as a teachers' manual for a progressive set of etudes/pieces for string orchestra called *22 Groove Studies for Strings*. In the heading of most chapters in this book, you will find an indication of the Groove Study that corresponds to that chapter. In the score, the heading of each Groove Study indicates the related chapter of *The Strum Bowing Method*. The score and instrumental parts for *22 Groove Studies for Strings* are available separately.

A highly abridged version of the material in *The Strum Bowing Method* is included in the instrumental books to help guide students through the complete Strum Bowing curriculum.

Most of the Groove Studies have "lyrics." I use the term loosely because they are usually either the bow direction or some other similar learning reinforcement. Sometimes pitches are indicated, but often, as in the case of saying the bow direction while playing non-pitched Chops, just saying the words out loud is all that is intended. If the Groove Studies are programmed in concerts, conductors should feel free to leave the lyrics out. Or not.

Acknowledgements

This book is an assemblage of collective wisdom. So much of what I've written are words that others have said to me. My heartfelt appreciation to my inspiring friends and trusted colleagues whose patience and good judgment I've imposed upon, who have helped me choose the right terminology and notation, have encouraged, advised, commented on, made suggestions for and/or proofread this book and have come up with so many great ideas that are included here. Much of the wisdom comes from other people, for which I am grateful and for which you should be, too, including:

Darol Anger, my big brother from the Turtle Island String Quartet, who has the best sense of time of anyone I've ever met, is completely telepathic, who taught me how to Chop, how to deal with life on the road and who continues to be an inspiration to me and to so many; **David Wallace**, chair of the string department at Berklee College of Music, the godparent of this book, who encouraged me for years to finish it and whose generous time, tireless energy, good vibes and countless tactfully delivered suggestions and advice have made this book so much better than it ever would have been otherwise; my manager, **Brian Horner**, who has helped with every stage of this process; innovative educator, author and violinist **Julie Lyonn Lieberman**, whose countless hours and devotion to truth, vision and grammar have helped to make sense out of my overwritten ideas; my daughter, **Louisa Silverman**, whose mastery of language, logical thinking and editing skills makes all that college tuition well worth it; graphic artist **Austin Gray**, who patiently turned this instruction manual into a work of art; painter **Rachel Kice**, whose gorgeous work reminds us that beauty is why we bother; **Casey Driessen**, who worked long and hard with me to find a consensus among alternative style string teachers about all this new notational territory for ghosts, Chops, etc, and who takes Chopping to a whole other level; **Mark Wood**, who got me started on the 6-string path, and who has done more for the electric violin than anyone as a player, instrument builder and through his Electrify Your Strings program and Mark Wood Rock Orchestra Camp; **Richard Greene**, the guy who started the whole Chop thing way back when with Bill Monroe; the multi-genre creativity and good humor of cellist **Mike Block**; Irish fiddler extraordinaire **Martin Hayes**; **Christian Howes**, who brings authentic jazz playing to the alternative strings world through his podcasts and educational programs; rock violin crushers **Joe Deninzon**, **Earl Maneein**, **Chuck Bontrager** and **Alex DePue**; classical/heavy metal (yes!) virtuoso **Rachel Barton Pine**; violinist/composer **Daniel Bernard Roumain**; string orchestra composer/arranger/guru **Bob Phillips**, who had so much helpful advice; **Mark O'Connor**, whose playing and camps brought together so many amazing players of different styles in a collaborative spirit; my TISQ mate **Danny Seidenberg**; the Suzuki pedagogue **Pam Wiley** and her rhythm-friendly **American Music System**; jazz educator/arranger **Bert Ligon**, a guitar player who has written so many great string arrangements that he's become an honorary string player; Belmont University's Juilliard-trained **Elisabeth Small**, jazz phenom **Billy Contreras** and Grammy winning fiddler **Tammy Rogers-King**; high school education specialists **Daryl Silberman** and **Carrie Turner** and all the other great players and teachers I may have accidentally omitted. I've learned so much from all of you!

A lifetime of gratitude to **Debbra Wood Schwartz** and **Morris Gomberg** at the Chicago Musical College, and **Lewis Kaplan** and **Ivan Galamian** at The Juilliard School, all of whom taught me how to play the violin properly a long time ago; to **my parents**, who drove me to a lot of violin lessons; to **my wife and kids** who have cheerfully and encouragingly put up with this whole I've-decided-to-write-a-book thing; to all the innovative choppers and groove-players out there, the countless street performers, club musicians and bedroom YouTubers who are often the real leading edge of contemporary string playing, pushing the possibilities of string instruments in inspirational ways that defy easy analysis and force open the minds of old school players like myself, teaching us old dogs new tricks; and to all my students who really taught me better than anyone how to get this across in a useful way.

Part I:
The Strum
The Heart of the Groove

An Introduction to Strum Bowing

Strum Bowing is such a simple concept that it can be explained in one phrase: using a bow like you're strumming a guitar.

Strum Bowing—The Heart of the Groove

Strum Bowing is a method for teaching string players how to authentically play the rhythms of contemporary popular music. Technically, it is the act of physicalizing the subdivision of the beat with the bow. Strum Bowing is how a string player's bow arm naturally responds to a groove—it's how you dance with your bow.

Strum Bowing is the act of physicalizing the subdivision of the beat with the bow.

The strum may show up as an obvious rhythmic part of a song—possibly a *Chop* pattern that imitates a drum or rhythm guitar part. Or, it may manifest itself more subtly as an implied groove that comes from your inner drummer, present not only in your musical imagination but also physically in your bow arm. This inner drummer may influence your choice of bow direction and your use of accents and *ghost notes* (pitches or percussive noises that are barely audible) even in melodic lines.

In addition to learning the Chop and what I call *3-D Strum* patterns, an important aspect of Strum Bowing is the development of your inner drummer—the internalized, physicalized sense of pulse and rhythm. You will learn to become more aware of the pulse and groove even in classical music. (See Ch. 20: "The Rhythm of Melody—Bringing Strum Bowing into Classical Playing.") This process of physicalizing a groove will make you a better player... and possibly a better dancer.

Even though this method is about bowing, the concepts of physicalizing the subdivision and listening to your inner drummer are just as effective with *pizzicato*, and therefore, equally important for bass players to understand.

Because this area of string playing is relatively new, there hasn't yet been a broad, overarching understanding of how these different rhythmic pop and folk styles are connected, nor has there been a method for teaching rhythm string playing in a comprehensive way that includes them all.

A Simple Unified Approach

The reason **Strum Bowing** is so effective with students of all ages is because Strum Bowing is so easy to learn. It doesn't focus on the complexity of rhythm; it focuses on the simplicity. This way of reframing string playing connects all the different bow techniques—Chops, shuffles, percussive hits, slaps and pizz techniques—in all genres of music by focusing on the common thread linking all grooves: the subdivision of the beat.

The human tendency to subdivide, to make a fast and consistent physical motion out of a slower pulse, is not only the common element in grooves of all genres, it's also what distinguishes one genre's sound from another's. When we articulate 16 sixteenth notes in a bar, for instance, it gives us much more material to work with in shaping a groove to fit a particular style than if we only play the four quarter notes. And this is where strumming comes in.

Strumming is simply playing the subdivision.

Physics Always Wins

Strum Bowing is essential in order to work with the natural physics of using a bow instead of against it. Bowing tends toward consistent back and forth motions, rather than the uneven accents of most grooves.

> **Subdivision**
>
> 1. The act of dividing a pulse evenly into smaller increments. For instance, a quarter note can be divided into four sixteenth notes.
>
> 2. A fraction of a pulse. For instance, one of the four sixteenth notes in a quarter note.

Moving your arm back and forth will naturally tend toward equilibrium, like a pendulum, and a lopsided rhythm will naturally begin to even out over time. Our bodies tend to move evenly, rather than starting and stopping suddenly. Just imagine trying to walk in this rhythm:

Ex. Intro A

You will soon find yourself walking like this:

Ex. Intro B

...and after a few minutes, like this:

Ex. Intro C

Your arms function the same way. Your bow arm naturally wants to play even back and forth strokes. But, thanks to the miracle of subdivision, grooves have many uneven accents. If we try to play only those accents with back and forth strokes, we are breaking the law of equilibrium and trying to get our bow to start and stop in an unnatural way. This is what happens when we try to play the uneven accents of a groove with as-it-comes bowing. First of all, we end up accenting things not necessarily because we want them accented but just because we have to move the bow faster. It is impossible to fully overcome the physics that causes one bow stroke to be louder than another when it has to travel the same distance in a third of the time.

Ex. Intro D

Like uneven walking, uneven bowing does not encourage rhythmic accuracy. Pretty soon the pattern above will turn into this:

Ex. Intro E

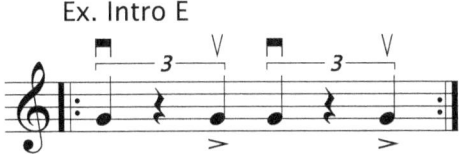

That's why drummers and rhythm guitar players—whose job it is to keep time—establish a constant subdivision that they maintain with a natural, simple physical motion, such as a strum. The beauty of this system is that once you establish these subdivisions, you can accent any of them that you like and change those accents on the fly without disturbing the pulse. (See Ch. 2: "The Grid—The Structure of Grooves.")

What's the Difference Between the Strum and the Chop?

The Strum Bowing method includes the Chop, which has become ubiquitous among alternative-style string players. But, Strum Bowing is a broader concept that refers to the underlying rhythmic motor that powers the Chop and other strokes, such as the shuffle and ghost notes: the subdivision.

There are more and more string teachers who have learned how to Chop and are teaching that Chop to their students. Often, the student will learn a specific pattern that will work for a particular song or style, but the pattern may not apply to other songs or styles. So, the student is left with a cool but ultimately disappointing gimmick rather than a deeper understanding and ability to groove on their instrument.

Strum Bowing is a broader concept that refers to the underlying rhythmic motor that powers the Chop and other strokes, such as the shuffle and ghost notes: the subdivision.

Introduction

String players should use their bodies to discover rhythms, rather than relying only on their brains to learn patterns.

If that student is very motivated, they may try to learn several of these different patterns, often from different teachers who may specialize in one musical genre, such as bluegrass or Celtic, but not another, such as rock. All these different patterns are complicated to learn because there are endless variations and mutations, some being quite similar. There are way too many possible patterns for most people to memorize. As a result, it's common for players to slip into a rut, using the same handful of Chop patterns they've learned, unsure how to broaden their limited vocabulary in an interesting way.

String players should not have to memorize complex patterns in order to play grooves. They should learn how to use their bodies to discover rhythms, rather than relying only on their brains to learn patterns.

Variety and Improvisation

The significance and power of Strum Bowing is the rhythmic flexibility it gives you to easily and intuitively morph from one pattern to another without disrupting the rhythmic flow. This enables you to play in many different musical genres and to easily and spontaneously add variety and subtle changes to a groove. Strumming is a simple form of rhythmic improvisation, which is the key to good rhythm playing. (See Ch. 11: "Variety is the Spice of Grooves—The Power of the Strum.")

Birth of the Strum

The Strum Bowing concept comes from the way guitar players strum. They maintain a constant motion with their right hand even when not all the notes are sounded, using accents and ghosts to bring out an endless variety of grooves. (See Ch. 4: "Ghost Notes: How to *Not* Play An Instrument.")

Here's the quick story of my Eureka! moment. One day, I was watching a band on TV. The guitar player was strumming an acoustic guitar when my phone rang. I muted the TV and watched him strum while I chatted for a few minutes. Then, I hung up the phone and unmuted the TV. The guitar player was still strumming away as he had been before, but now it was a different tune and a different groove. Huh? With the sound off, the strumming of both tunes looked exactly the same. His right hand had never stopped moving up and down the whole time. Ohhhh…

Play the Subdivision

A light bulb went on over my head, and I realized that this was the key to teaching the chop and all that groovy rhythm stuff I played with my rock bands and Turtle Island String Quartet: all of the subdivisions are played in some way, not just the accents. So simple!

It seems too obvious, but the truth is that playing the subdivisions of the beat is the common thread in all groove-based music and the missing link in contemporary string teaching. It's the reason many string players can't groove. Yet.

Playing the subdivisions is a simple concept, but it's deceptively difficult to put into practice, especially for classical string players. There are 3 reasons for this.

- First, playing rhythm is not a native part of classical string instruction, which focuses more on melody and virtuosity. Strings are so difficult to play that the focus is on tone and articulation in the bow arm and intonation, accuracy and speed in the left hand. Since strings are generally not used as chordal instruments, strumming chords to keep time for a singer or dancer is not something we typically learn how to do.

- Second, we're taught how to play notes, but we're never taught how to *not* play notes—we're taught how to accent but not how to ghost.

Playing the subdivisions of the beat is the common thread in all groove-based music and the missing link in contemporary string teaching.

- And third, we only play what's on the page, and we aren't allowed to add anything that's not written by a composer. So, string players rarely learn how to improvise even simple rhythmic variations.

However, subdivision is foundational to folk fiddling, a style in which the violin is sometimes the only accompaniment for dances. The melodies in many fiddle tunes consist of a fairly constant subdivision of the beat, resulting in a bow stroke commonly referred to as a shuffle.

While few classical methods focus on these rhythmic techniques, the Mark O'Connor Method books and Pat Wiley's American Music System bring some of that inherent rhythm into early violin pedagogy.

But, to play the subdivision, first you have to find it. It's the smallest note value of the groove—the smallest particle of the groove, if you will. With a nod to my forbears in the world of theoretical physics, I have named this particle the *Groovon*.

The significance and power of Strum Bowing is the rhythmic flexibility it gives you to easily and intuitively morph from one pattern to another without disrupting the rhythmic flow.

1. The Groovon
The Smallest Particle of the Groove

Groovon

1. The smallest particle of a rhythmic groove; the smallest usable subdivision of the beat; a Groovon is to a beat what protons and neutrons are to atoms. (The Groovon was first identified by the pseudo-physiomusicologist, Artov D. Grööve.)

2. A good rhythmic flow, as in "get your groovon."

Just as atoms are made up of smaller elements, such as protons, neutrons and electrons, a beat is made up of what I call Groovons. These are the smallest subdivisions of a groove.

The subdivision of the pulse is the common thread of all grooves in all genres.

You can subdivide time just as you can subdivide space. You can divide a pulse in music into smaller sub-pulses just as you can divide an inch into half and quarter inches. You can take a quarter note and divide it into two 8th notes or four 16th notes, and so on.

Theoretically, you can divide a beat infinitely, but what we are concerned with here is finding the smallest practical part of the beat: the fastest subdivision you hear in the song.

This subdivision can show up on many different instruments. It could be the strumming of a guitar; the congas, bongos or the shaker in the percussion; an arpeggiated keyboard riff; or a fast moving lyric or vocal part. Sometimes the Groovons are fully played, and sometimes they're barely implied. If there's a pulse, there's a subdivision of it, and if you want to be able to groove with a song, the first thing you have to do is find the Groovon.

Continuous Groovons

In many pop songs you can hear the Groovons played more or less continuously by either one instrument or a combination of instruments.

We might look to the drums for the Groovons, but although the drums are always playing part of the groove, they are not always playing the fastest part of it. In a lot of rock and pop music, the fastest thing in the drum may be eighth notes in the hi-hat, and the smaller subdivision may be in the guitar, keyboard or vocal.

> **Pulse**
>
> The beat. For instance, in 4/4 time, there are four pulses per measure.

Guitars

We've heard singer/songwriters so often that the strumming guitar accompanying a voice is possibly the most iconic sound of pop music. One classic example of this is The Eagles' "Best of My Love." When you strum a guitar, no matter what tempo or style of song it may be, the strumming motion is essentially the same—down up down up, continuously. Each stroke of the strum is the smallest particle of the beat, or the Groovon. "You've Got A Friend" by James Taylor has an arpeggiated guitar part playing the Groovons, as does "Sweet Child of Mine" by Guns and Roses. U2's "Pride (In the Name of Love)" starts out with a continuous strum riff in the guitar that also has strong syncopated accents emphasizing certain Groovons over others.

In rock music, the Groovons are often in the electric guitar. Sometimes this will be a simple repeated note, called "chugging." These chugs are easy to accent in different ways, making them very similar to Strum Bowing.

"Whole Lotta Love" by Led Zeppelin starts with a clear example of chugging Groovons in the electric guitar. A similar guitar-based stream of Groovons drives "Eye of the Tiger" by Survivor. Metallica's "Master of Puppets" also puts the Groovons in the guitar.

On the funkier side of things, one of the clearest examples of

> **Syncopation**
>
> Accenting a normally unaccented up beat. It usually has the feeling of anticipating the following beat.

continuous Groovons in the guitar is the rhythm guitar in Kool & the Gang's "Celebration." Nile Rogers' rhythm guitar part in Daft Punk's "Get Lucky" is a perfect example of a partly ghosted rhythm guitar part that drives a tune. The rhythm guitar in the Mick Ronson/Bruno Mars tune "Uptown Funk" does the same but more sparsely. David Bowie's "Modern Love" starts with a guitar riff of almost completely continuous Groovons with accents on the song's main rhythmic riff.

Drums

Sometimes the Groovons are most noticeable in the drums.

"Straight Outta Compton" by NWA starts out with continuous Groovons in the hi-hat that give a relentlessness drive to the track. Taylor Swift's "Shake It Off" starts with a drum groove that shares the Groovons among the kick and snare drums and the drum stick hits. Then, notice how the saxophone comes in with a riff that repeats a single pitch, creating the sax version of chugging. "Black Magic Woman" by Santana is a great example of how many percussion instruments combine in Latin music to create a continuous quilt of Groovons. Michael Jackson's "Wanna Be Startin' Somethin'" starts with "somethin'" on the drums: drum machines, actually—a combination of hi-hat and shaker sounds that create a continuous series of Groovons.

Keyboard

Sometimes, the Groovons are in a keyboard part or, especially in electronic dance music, in a synthesizer or manipulated drum loop.

Elton John starts "Rocket Man" on solo piano and doesn't need anyone else to get the groove across. Chords are arpeggiated, notes are accented and rhythm and harmony are balanced. "Sweet Dreams (Are Made of This)" by the Eurythmics is driven by a synth bass line. Skrillex's "Scary Monsters and Nice Sprites" gets the track off to a hypnotic start with the continuous Groovons in the synth-drums. Michael Jackson's "Human Nature" starts with continuous Groovons in the keyboard. The

Groovons then move to the rhythm guitar with a great example of ghosting in a rhythm riff.

Saxophone and Trumpet

In jazz, the Groovons are often hinted at in the ride cymbal and emphasized in the snare drum. But they show up the most continuously in the solo instruments, which are often playing streams of subdivisions. For example, in Coltrane's "Giant Steps," the solo instruments carry the rhythm.

Implied Groovons

What makes the Groovon a little trickier to recognize in many tunes is that, more often than not, it is not continuously played. It is often implied more than actually played, the way a cartoonist might indicate a few bricks to suggest an entire brick wall. A syncopated horn riff, for example, may consist of only one or two notes, but because of where those accents are placed, they can imply a subdivision. The rhythm in Ex. 1A from Prince's "1999" does not play the subdivision continuously, but it's all we need. Our imagination fills in the missing sixteenths.

The Groovon is often implied more than actually played, the way a cartoonist might indicate a few bricks to suggest an entire brick wall.

Ex. 1A

In Michael Jackson's "Billie Jean," the fastest note in the bass and drums is the eighth note. The only place that hints at a smaller subdivision is the vocals. It's not until the 2nd chorus that the rhythm guitar comes in with sparse sixteenths and then brings them forward with the repeated riff. This is a perfect example of how the Groovons can be powerful when they are implied and not fully realized and how bringing the Groovons forward heightens the energy of the tune.

Whether it's more present, driving the song forward, or more implied and simmering under the surface, the Groovon supplies the energy of the song.

The Groovon supplies the energy of the song.

James Brown's "Papa's Got A Brand New Bag" has the Groovons just whispering in the hi-hat with a hard swing. But you almost don't even realize the Groovons are there until the rhythm guitar hits that iconic strum riff.

In ACDC's "Back in Black," the hi-hat is playing eighth notes, but the guitar is playing a riff that includes a few sixteenth notes. (By the way, just to hear the difference, here the Groovons are not swung.) Even though the sixteenths are not continuous as they are in a song like "Eye of the Tiger," the feeling of them is implied. The vocal actually has a lot of the subdivision. This is especially true of a lot of rap and hip-hop, where the vocal may have the fastest-moving rhythm of the song.

Vocal

Beyonce's "Single Ladies (Put a Ring on It)" has a sparse beat, but the vocal drives the rhythm. "Lose Yourself" by Eminem has eighths in the drums, but the vocal has all the subdivision. Some rap vocals even double-time the subdivision, as in Eminem's "Rap God."

The groove of a song may be a combination of many instruments, each playing their own fragment of Groovons in a rhythmic dialogue shared by several different instruments. This is true of most Latin dance music. It's also true of Prince's "1999." Listen and see if you can find all the different instruments that are playing the sixteenth note Groovons.

Groovons are usually sixteenth notes, but if the tempo is fast enough, they will be the eighth notes, as in Outkast's "Hey Ya!"

In a Melody

Subdivisions are often implied even in an unaccompanied melody. In the following melody, the smallest particle is the 16th note.

Ex. 1B

(It's a small particle, after all.)

In this next melody, the smallest particle is the thirty-second note. To play it accurately, you need to imagine your inner drummer playing eight thirty-second notes in each beat.

Ex. 1C

The Groovon is Always Right

Since the Groovon divides the beat into smaller parts, it has greater power to influence the song. It controls the tempo of the song because the listener's ear will identify the tempo by following those faster subdivisions rather than slower rhythms that may be played by another instrument. In other words, the listener will get a sense of tempo from a sixteenth note pattern in the hi-hat rather than from the bass player's quarter notes. I tell students, "The drummer is always right" because even if the drummer is rushing or dragging the tempo, you have to play with them or you will sound like you're wrong. For example, a bass player may be playing quarter notes perfectly in time, but if the drummer is rushing the sixteenth notes, it will sound like the bass is behind the beat. The Groovon controls the tempo.

The Groovon also controls the style. The more notes or rhythmic figures played per beat, the more ways there are to add variety. The last sixteenth note of a bar can be accented to bring out a syncopated feel, or the second sixteenth note can be accented to bring out a samba feel, etc. Subdivisions can be swung for jazz and hip-hop or played straight for a Latin or rock style. There are many things that characterize a genre, such as instrumentation or tempo, but one of the most crucial aspects of any musical style is the character of the rhythmic groove. So, the way the Groovon is played can determine the style of the song.

> **Swing**
>
> The unequal subdivision of a pulse in which the first note is typically twice as long as the second, creating a triplet. The amount of swing can vary from a subtle unevenness to a "hard" swing.

The Groovon controls the tempo.

Because they who control the Groovon control their own destiny.

String players are often captive to whatever other instruments define as the rhythmic environment. They typically have to follow whoever sets the pace or tone with limited means of defining their own rhythmic/stylistic world. It's crucial for string players to learn how to groove in order to become functioning members of the rhythm section. Because they who control the Groovon control their own destiny.

C'mon string players! We're taking it back!

Play
Shake It 'Til You Make It

- Choose any tune. Take a small shaker or a box of mints or just pretend you're strumming a guitar, and try to locate the Groovons in the tune. They're the fastest rhythm you hear. (Spoiler alert: they're almost always sixteenth notes.)

- Beatbox the drum part of the song.

- Play air guitar while you beatbox.

- Now air-bow it like you're the Paganini of the Groovon.

- Repeat with another tune.

The Groovon

Thriving in the Rhythm Section

THERE ARE MANY CHALLENGES facing classically trained string players who are making the transition to dance-based music. One challenge is learning to be member of the rhythm section. Aside from the technical issues, there is the problem of learning to love a part that appears so repetitive. On paper, rhythm section parts may look like an exercise in redundancy, especially compared to the variety found in the melodic line. But in reality, playing in the rhythm section can be subtle and complex. It can also be the most fun you'll ever have making music.

The rhythm section is a group of people working together, driving the band, making listeners want to dance, clap along or, at the very least, bob their heads in time with the groove. Being part of the engine that propels the music is the ultimate ensemble experience.

I think of a rhythm section as clockworks with lots of gears, each a different size, all fitting together flawlessly to keep perfect time. Each player is responsible for keeping a gear turning at exactly the right speed. If the tiniest grain of sand gets into the gears everything will fall apart.

Great rhythm section players often go beyond the groove-making machinery by adding and subtracting parts for musical emphasis. There is a lively conversation going on all the time. One player adds an unexpected accent, another joins in. That accent develops into a conversation. New ideas are created. The exchange builds with a big crescendo and finishes off the 8-bar phrase with a flourish.

It is thrilling to be part of a rhythm section that can respond instantaneously to a new idea—from within either the section or the soloist—and incorporate that idea into the groove. This sort of playing is the pinnacle of ensemble work: listening to each other and participating in a collaborative and dynamic musical environment in real time while keeping the groove strong and solid.

My first rhythm section experience was in a 3-piece string band that played traditional Hungarian music. I played off-beats to the bass player's down-beats. The third part was the melody. Written out, my part was the ultimate snooze. But, playing it was a rich pleasure. Fitting that off-beat into exactly the right moment between the down-beats was a thrill. Knowing that the melody and the dancers would both collapse if those gears didn't mesh faultlessly added to the excitement. Our sets started at a slow tempo and gradually sped up until the last group of tunes was at lightning speed. Maintaining the groove over a long period of time and through accelerating tempos was deeply satisfying. Since my time in that band, I've had the opportunity to participate in many rhythm sections that play lots of different musical styles. Each style comes with a unique groove and each groove is a fabulous musical adventure.

Creating the groove is a different kind of joy than playing the melody, but they are deeply connected. Groove playing is a great way to inform your melodic playing. If you have spent some time working on the groove, your melodic playing will be richer and more connected to the piece as a whole.

Enjoy generating the groove!

Mimi Rabson,
Assoc. Prof., Berklee College of Music
www.mimirabson.com

2. The Grid
The Structure of Grooves

Grid

A consistent framework that helps keep rhythms evenly aligned; a rhythm ruler; a.k.a. The Groovon Grid.

The consistent down/up motion of strumming creates a rhythmic grid. In the diagram below, each line of the grid represents a Groovon, a subdivision of the beat.

Ex. 2A

On strings, a groove is a pattern of down and up bows. Some of the strokes are accented, and some are not, depending on the rhythmic pattern you want to create. Jazz players call the unaccented notes ghost notes. (See Ch. 4: "Ghost Notes—How to *Not* Play An Instrument.") Each groove has a different pattern of accents and ghosts. By subtly accenting and ghosting in different degrees and varying those patterns, we can create an infinite possibility of grooves.

Although there are as many gradations of stressed and unstressed notes as a player's technique allows, for now, let's just work in black and white with either accents or ghosts. Let's imagine we are playing a snare drum. This rhythm:

Ex. 2B

... could be represented this way as a grid:

Ex. 2C

The grid shows us exactly where those accents land in relation to each other and precisely how many evenly spaced subdivisions exist between them. The musical example (Ex. 2B) shows only the accented notes. The grid in Ex. 2C demonstrates what is actually happening in a strum: all the subdivisions are physicalized either as accents or as ghosts. A strum doesn't stop in between accents. It keeps moving consistently all the time and functions as a grid to keep the rhythm properly aligned. The musical notation in example 2B is actually incomplete, since you play extra notes to fill in the rests in the groove with strum bowing.

If we notated it more precisely, it would look like this:

Ex. 2D

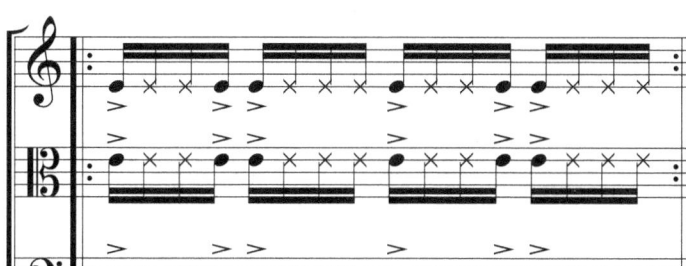

Ghost Notes

The unstressed notes in a groove; dropped notes; nearly inaudible pitched or unpitched sounds; the opposite of accents.

Filling In the Blanks

Vernacular styles often use a kind of musical shorthand. We might see Ex 2B, but we would be expected to play it like Ex. 2D. Musical notation is like "map view" where you only see the important features like roads and landmarks. But in real life, music is like "satellite view," a photo including more of the details of reality.

So, when we strum, we are playing the main accents of the groove, but we are also filling in the blanks by ghosting the unstressed subdivisions. These added ghost notes serve to keep us lined up accurately and keep our place on the grid. That's why I sometimes refer to these ghosted Groovons as placekeeper notes. (See Ch. 5: "Placekeeper Notes—Locking to the Grid") They are not written in the music, but by creating a rhythmic grid of steady up and down strokes with a strum, we're automatically adding placekeeper notes between the accents. We're turning map view into satellite view; turning a written rhythm into a groove.

> **Groove**
>
> A consistent subdivision of the pulse defined by a pattern of accented and ghosted notes.

The Energy Grid

The grid helps to give us rhythmic precision, and that translates to the listener as musical energy. Sloppy rhythm is like a lazy athlete.

As string players, we are often playing melodies, so we may tend to underestimate the importance of locking in to a grid when we are asked to play rhythm. We are more accustomed to a sort of "emotional grid," sculpted artfully to push and pull the tempo for maximum effect. Counting evenly while playing passages like this is not only practically impossible to do, it may be deliberately avoided in order to create more of an emotional effect. You might think of this style of melodic playing like dramatic acting but with an instrument.

But when we play rhythmically with the intention of creating or adding to a groove, counting and feeling the pulse is crucial. The grid—expressed as a steady strum—is always there. It's built into the very concept of a groove.

Now, you may be very highly trained and believe that your sense of rhythm is so accurate that you don't need the "crutch" of physicalizing the grid with a strum. But ignore the grid at your own peril. It's certainly possible to play just the accents of a groove without adding all the placekeepers in between, but you are much more likely to drift off the grid and lose your rhythmic vigor. Why make it harder on yourself? Besides, all those little percussive ticks and clicks that percolate along in between the accents are really what give a groove all its coolness and character. It's all in the ghosting.

Sloppy rhythm is like a lazy athlete.

Precision on a Human Scale

We are rarely as precise as we like to think we are.

Try to draw dots exactly two inches apart across a large piece of paper. You might get one right, but you almost certainly won't get them all right. But if I give you some graph paper with pre-drawn guidelines every quarter inch, you would be able to do it perfectly. Just as we divide space into inches or centimeters with a ruler, we divide time into beats with a metronome. If I ask you to clap every two seconds, you might get it exactly right once or twice. But if I divide each second into four equal clicks, you can easily do the math and clap once every eight clicks. 100% precision.

The grid becomes more necessary as the scale becomes larger. For instance, imagine I now ask you to place markers exactly fifty inches apart across a football field without any ruler or tape measure. You probably won't get a single one right. And if I ask you to clap exactly every twenty seconds, you probably won't get it right even once.

You can tap your toe pretty accurately twice a second. Slow that down to once every five seconds and you lose the continuity right away. If the beats are too far apart, it's difficult to know whether you are speeding up or slowing down. In order to make rhythm useful, we need to bring it into human scale, to connect it with the organic way our bodies work.

This is why it's so important to physicalize the Groovon, the smallest particle of the beat, with a continuous strum: a strum is a human-sized motion that we can rely on to be steady. (See Ch. 7: "The Dance of the Groove—Physicalizing the Beat.")

In order to make rhythm useful, we need to bring it into human scale, to connect it with the organic way our bodies work.
A strum is a human-sized motion that we can rely on to be steady.

The Grid

The Future of Strings in the 21st Century

BACK IN THE 1980's there were 2 Juilliard maniacs plotting to take the electric guitar off the rock and roll pedestal and return that status to the rightful owner, the violin. We all know that Paganini was truly the first rock star:)

Enter Tracy Silverman and Mark Wood.

Both Tracy and I inspired and motivated each other to reach higher with our goals in the electric violin world. Of course, we both respected Jascha Heifetz and all the great solo violinists of the past 200 years. But we both also revered Jimi Hendrix, Prince, the Beatles, Led Zeppelin and other bands just as much! We wanted to rock!

So we both shared our adventures with each other over the years. And here we are. After

30+ years in the music industry as "non-classical" string players, where do we stand now as a string community and how has our music and perceptions changed?

Tracy and I have spent many hundreds of hours preaching about the importance of integrating a broad approach to music making on string instruments. Strings must not be taught from a narrow viewpoint but with all the infinite capabilities, expressions, depth of feelings and emotions that define music and which is the reason we all became musicians! When I give my workshops, I tell the students, "You are not violin players, viola players, cello players, or bass players…you are musicians first!"

Our future string classes must compete with the other cutting edge and innovative classrooms in content, experience and engagement. We are competing with sports, computer classes, rocketry classes, chess classes and innovative academics. We can't have antiquated teaching methods. We must look critically at our pedagogy, innovate, and really use the music as the prime force of motivation. Students must be able to not only experience and learn about our 400 year old tradition of incredible music, but they must also find their voice and themselves in the present day.

Music is a conversation and a language skill. A great melody is like a great sentence. Just teaching the notes and notation on the page is like teaching only the alphabet and never allowing students to connect those building blocks into beautiful forms of personal communication. This is the power of improvisation!

For string programs to have a fighting chance, we must incorporate technology, improvisation and American styles with our traditional classical pedagogy. If not, kids will just quit and join band or go play soccer.

Tracy and I spearheaded this movement over 40 years ago. Rock on Tracy!!

Mark Wood
7-String Electric Violinist, founder of Wood Violins, Mark Wood Rock Orchestra Camp, Electrify Your Strings
www.markwoodmusic.com

3. Strum 101
Getting your Groovon

See: Groove Study 1

OK, now that you know all about Groovons and grids, let's have a try at our first groove.

First, get the groove in your voice. Sing this rhythm. You can say "Dah" or "Bop" or any nonsense syllable you like.

What would you play if you were playing a shaker?

Now, let's find the Groovon. What is the smallest particle of this groove? What would you play if you were playing a shaker?

In the example below, the Groovon is written as hollow note heads to indicate air strums, so don't put your bow on the string yet. In fact, you don't need to hold your bow at all. You can just air strum sixteenth notes like this:

Continue to air strum the Groovon, and let's try to sing the rhythm from Ex. 3A at the same time.

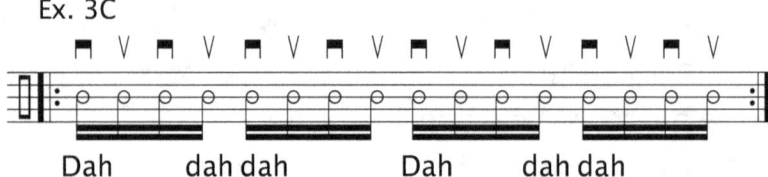

Next, change the lyric from "dah dah dah" to the bow direction lyrics as shown below. Don't stop air strumming!

Ex. 3D

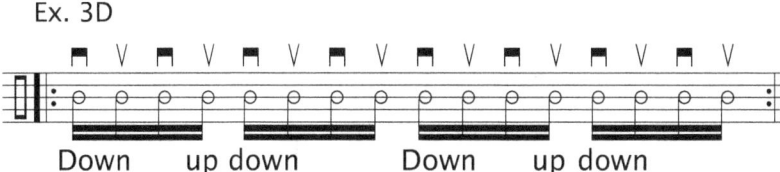

Down   up down   Down   up down

Now, while you air strum and say the bow directions out loud, place your bow on the string, and start playing the Groovons. Let your voice help you emphasize the accents. Make sure you're actually saying, "Down, up down" out loud, not just in your head.

Ex. 3E

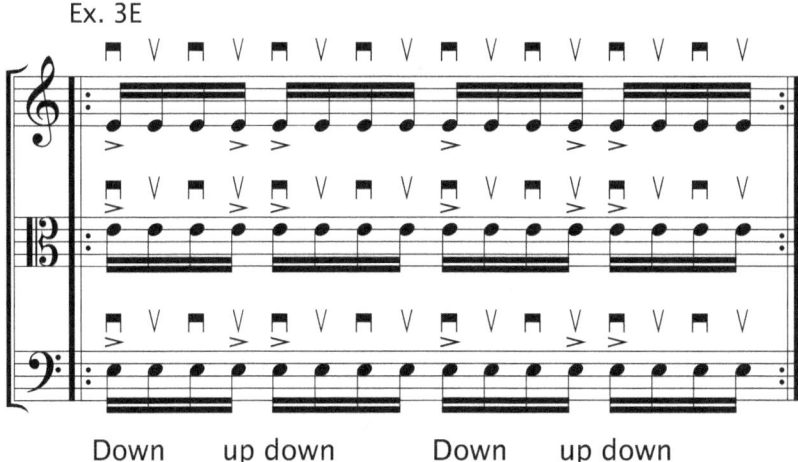

Down   up down   Down   up down

If you're like most string players, when you finally put the bow on the string and play the last example, you will be hearing a lot of repeated E droning between the accents. That's OK for now. We'll learn how to ghost in the next chapter.

Let's try it again but with a slightly cooler rhythm.

First, get the groove in your voice. Sing this without playing:

Dah   dah dah   dah   dah   dah dah

Now let's get the groove in our bodies. Air strum the Groovon:

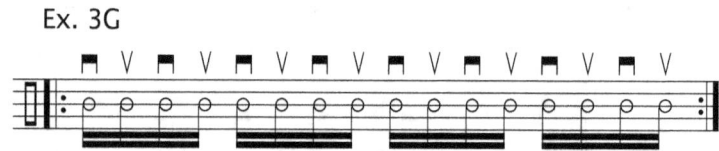

Let's put the two together. While you air strum, add your voice:

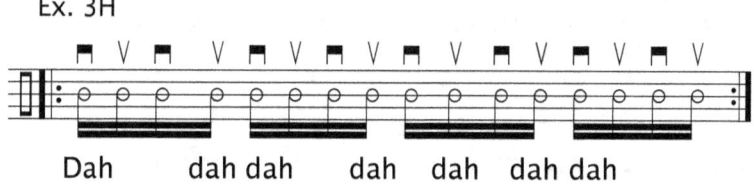

Dah   dah dah   dah   dah   dah dah

Next, swap the nonsense lyric for the bow direction lyric, still air strumming.

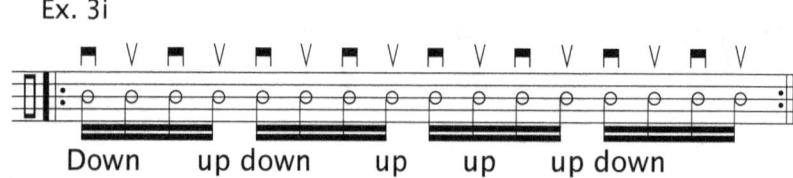

Down   up down   up   up   up down

And finally, put the bow on the string and keep singing the bow direction lyric:

Ex. 3J

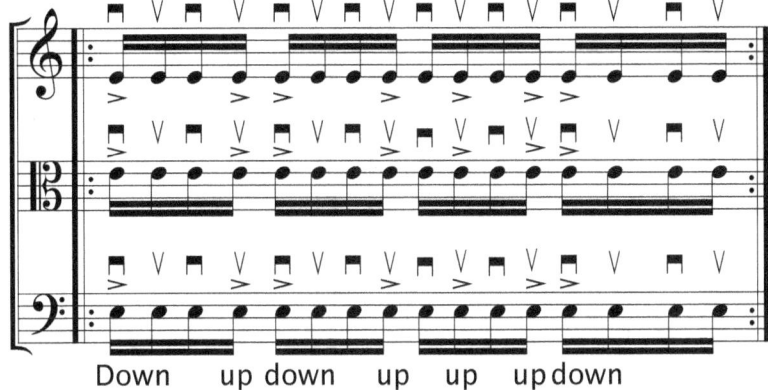

Down   up down   up   up   up down

Let your voice help your bow arm.

OK, that might have been a little challenging and difficult to put together, but we're going to break it down in the next few chapters and return to it in Chapter 8, "GPS: The Groove Proficiency System."

4. Ghost Notes
How to *Not* Play An Instrument

See: Groove Study 2, Groove Study 3, Groove Study 4

You may have spent years learning how to play beautiful notes on your instrument, but probably no one ever taught you how to *not* play notes.

Ghost notes are an exotic idea for many classical players. Classical string playing rarely uses this technique, so the idea of moving your bow without making sound—or making a non-pitched percussive sound—is not familiar to most string players.

As we've learned, a groove is defined as much by what you bring out as by what you drop, or ghost. But how do we do that?

Both hands work together to play ghost notes.

Right hand—tiny bow strokes with minimal bow pressure.
Left hand—muting: dampen the string by either
1. Laying your pinky across the string, or
2. Applying lighter finger pressure.

Both hands work together to play ghost notes.

Tiny Bow Strokes

The key to ghosting is to use very little bow. With tiny bow strokes, you can still use pressure to bring out accents cleanly, whereas with fuller bows, you would never be able to hide those ghosts.

Practice with tiny bow strokes less than an inch long, and see if you can lighten up the bow pressure on those ghost notes so much that you can make the bow glide over the string without producing any sound at all.

Focus not only on being light on the ghost notes but also on being heavy on the accents. Can you get a strong accent with very little bow? You will learn through practice how to adjust the pressure on the bow quickly and accurately enough that you will be able to grab the string for an accent and then release it for a ghost. Remember to use very small bows.

This technique of using as little bow as possible even when playing loud notes will be unusual for many classical players who may have been taught to use long bow strokes to get a big sound. But this ability to "squash" the bow a little, to get heavier while reducing the amount of bow, really helps support rhythmic precision. Get used to playing in the lower half of the bow where the weight of the bow will help you articulate rhythms. It will also help you get those raw horn-like tones when you play jazz.

> **Dampen**
>
> To mute the string by touching it lightly with a finger of the left hand without producing a harmonic.

Dampen the String

You can also dampen the string with your left hand to assist your bow hand.

There are two ways to do this:

1. Use your pinky to dampen the string:
Rest the side of your pinky lightly on the strings where it will not produce a natural harmonic. On violin and viola, your fourth finger will land on a natural harmonic in first position. You can place your fourth finger a little above or below that harmonic node to avoid the harmonic. The pinky is a reliable way to dampen the strings, but depending on the phrase you're playing, it may not be practical. So there is another way to dampen the strings.

2. Dampen the note by applying lighter finger pressure with your left hand:
Lighten up your finger pressure on whichever finger you're using so that the string is lightly muted but doesn't produce a harmonic. It can be difficult to prevent harmonics from ringing on notes where harmonics occur naturally. For instance,

the note G on the D string will become a harmonic when finger pressure is lighter, whereas the E below it will not. So the pinky dampening might be a good choice on the G to keep the harmonic from ringing. Using more than one finger can also help prevent harmonics.

Why not just alter the pitch of other fingers in order to avoid the natural harmonics, as you might with your pinky? Well, you could, of course. But it's not a good idea to distort your left hand position, especially in faster passages. This often leads to some questionable intonation issues. Generally, if you are just dropping a note or two in a jazz passage, for instance, you might use lighter finger pressure. But if you are focusing on playing more extended rhythmic patterns, the pinky might be better suited.

When ghosting, convenience is a high priority since the point is for the note to be less audible, and if it's awkward or difficult to play, it will most likely stand out instead of being inconspicuous. So do what seems easiest.

Over time, you'll be able to anticipate which notes require your pinky and which you can play with another finger. There is actually a pretty broad grey area between pressing the finger all the way down and playing a harmonic. It's possible, with a little practice, to find the sweet spot in between the two that allows you to dampen notes with any finger you choose without producing any natural harmonics or pitches. If you think of yourself as a percussionist playing a wooden percussion instrument with strings, you may discover all sorts of interesting non-pitched or semi-pitched sounds you can get out of these spruce and maple boxes.

Keep in mind that in order to learn how to ghost, I am asking you to keep your bow moving at all times in a strumming motion--to physicalize the Groovon--which results in percussive noise. Once you are familiar with the fundamentals of ghosting, however, you may want notes to disappear completely rather than articulate them with non-pitched percussive

You may discover all sorts of interesting non-pitched or semi-pitched sounds you can get out of these spruce and maple boxes.

sounds. In order to do that, you can either 1) take your bow off the string completely but continue to air strum in order to keep the rhythm locked to the grid, or 2) reduce the tiny bows to the point that you can rest the bow on the string silently and "think" the motion instead of actually doing it, possibly with a pulsing downward weight of your arm rather than a back and forth motion which produces a sound. It's important, however, to first become comfortable with the idea of a continuous motion with accents and ghosts and then scale that back to non-motion. Otherwise it's too easy to revert back to a more typical use of the bow that does not include the physicalized subdivisions which is necessary in order to lock to a grid.

Let's revisit the exercise from the last chapter and apply these new techniques:

Ex. 4A

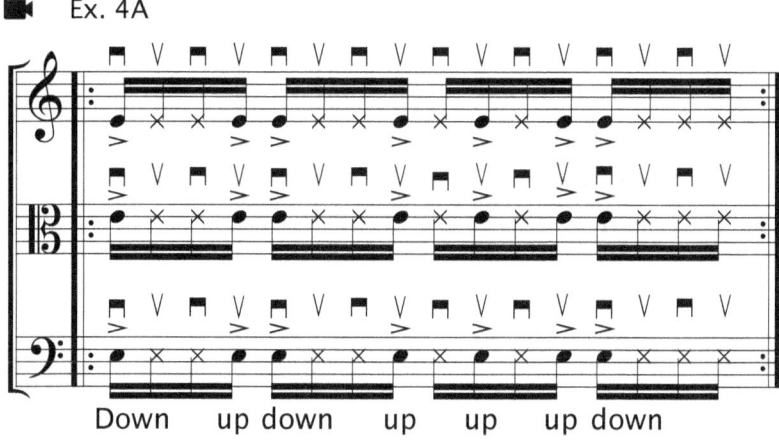

The bow is a very sophisticated tool capable of incredible nuances. Practice using varying amounts of pressure so that you can create endless gradations of ghosts or accents. Get a feel for transitioning from heavier ghost notes to lighter and lighter ghost notes until they disappear completely. Having control over many shades of ghosts gives you a wider palette of rhythmic color.

As you play Ex. 4A above, try moving back and forth through a spectrum of ghosting, as illustrated in the diagram below, Ex. 4B. Start out on the far left side of the chart playing all the sixteenth notes equally. Then, as you move to the right on the chart, start to bring out the accents more and more while also deemphasizing the ghost notes in between the accents. Finally, at the far right side of the chart, let the ghost notes disappear completely until you are left with only the accents being audible. Even though you only hear the accents, keep your bow moving back and forth for each sixteenth note. Remember to use tiny bow strokes and to dampen the ghost notes with your left hand.

Ex. 4B

All notes the same **Accents and ghosts**

Play

If you are a teacher, tell your students to imagine the shaded diagram in Ex. 4B on the floor. Then, using the rhythm from Ex. 4A. move back and forth across the floor diagram to indicate which level of ghosting the students should play.

Strum Bowing and the Modern Bow

TO GROOVE AND "STRUM" WITH A MODERN BOW, you should understand a few things about your bow's evolution and purpose. All plectrums were obviously built for strumming, but what about the modern bow?

Simply put, our modern bows (as refined by bow-maker François Tourte in the late eighteenth and early nineteenth century) were built to sustain and to produce a full, fat tone with a wide dynamic range.

The modern bow evolved to meet the reality that halls, audiences, and orchestras were all getting bigger. The music of the day was focusing more on harmonic complexity, rich sonorities, huge dynamic range and nuance, and long melodic lines. Generally speaking, pure rhythmic drive and complexity took a back seat.

Have you ever played with a Baroque bow? They're light. They articulate crisply and easily. Baroque bows and transitional bows of the Classical era typically produce a softer sound with a clear envelope, rather than a continuous, unwavering sustained tone. Is it any wonder that music of the Baroque sounds more articulate and dancelike than the Ro-

mantic music that arose with the heavier, Tourte-style bow?

So here's the dilemma: we've got these great modern bows that can produce a huge dynamic range, beautiful full sound, endless legato, and a plethora of articulations and bouncing strokes... but they're long, they're heavy (particularly at the tip and the frog), and compared to a pick, they can feel unwieldy and awkward when used for strumming. What to do?

One solution is to use a different kind of bow. At one time, Tracy Silverman was using half-size violin bows on his six-string electric violin to get an easier strum, especially in fast tempos and polyrhythmic grooves.

You can get a similar effect with short, early Baroque bows made of snake wood. However, this is a tradeoff: what you gain in ease of motion, you will lose in sustain and sonority. Moreover, the modern bow's extra weight really lends itself well to producing a good, solid chop. –Baroque sticks and half-sized sticks can't chop as well as a modern bow. (Score another victory for Tourte!)

In short, balance is your best friend. If you constantly balance your bow with flexible joints rather than clutching it with locked joints, your bow will become a natural extension of your arm. When you "air bow" without a stick, it's no effort to tap into the physical flow of the groovon. If your stick is balanced and your joints and muscles are free, you will have the exact same feeling.

Get to know your bow away from your instrument. Balance it on one of the fingers of your left hand to find the exact balance point. Play a few of the Groove Studies with your fingers touching the bow at the balance point rather than the frog to emphasize a sense of balance and lightness.

Next, move your fingers to the frog, but hold your bow completely vertically so the tip is pointed towards the sky and the weight of the bow is naturally supported by the earth's gravity, not your fingers. (This is a form of balance, too.) Gradually tip your bow more horizontally, and let your flexible fingers adjust so that everything remains in balance.

That's the feeling. Free fingers, balanced bow. Let gravity and your strings support the stick; you really don't need to squeeze at all.

Groove on! With a little careful practice, strumming with a balanced bow will start to feel just as natural as strumming with a pick.

Here's the exciting part: a modern bow has way more vast and subtle possibilities for articulation and dynamics than any plectrum ever will. You truly get the best of all worlds.

David "Doc" Wallace
Chair of the String Dept.,
Berklee College of Music
www.docwallacemusic.com

5. Placekeeper Notes
Locking to the Grid

See: Groove Study 5, Groove Study 6

> **Placekeeper Notes**
>
> Ghosted subdivisions that fill long notes or rests and keep you properly aligned on the grid.

We can think of the ghost notes we just finished working on as placekeeper notes. They are there to anchor the pulses exactly one beat apart from each other. They're like those quarter-inch guidelines on the graph paper we discussed in Chapter 2. (See Ch. 2: "The Grid—The Structure of Grooves.")

Your Inner Drummer

If you're creating or contributing to a groove, it's crucial to hear an inner drummer in your imagination. This inner drummer plays the Groovons, filling all the gaps between the accents of a groove. When someone plays with an uneven sense of rhythm, it's usually because they are not giving some notes or rests their full value, which almost always means they are not dancing to the beat of their inner drummer. That's probably why my teachers would say, "You're not counting. I can tell!"

If you are playing alone, make sure your inner drummer is on the gig too.

If you don't listen to your inner drummer, you may drift off the grid a bit. You may not line up with other musicians who are on the grid, such as the drums, bass or rhythm guitar. This kind of unintentional rhythmic inaccuracy weakens the groove. Sloppy rhythm is like bad muscle tone. It weakens the impact, draining the energy out of music and making it less compelling—whether in classical or popular genres—especially if it makes the pulse inconsistent. Placekeeper notes will help you stay on the grid and keep your grooves in shape.

Being deaf to your inner drummer is often symptomatic of not listening to the musicians you are playing with. Pay attention to whoever is playing the Groovon. Try to sync with their part. Remember, the Groovon is always right. If you are playing alone, make sure your inner drummer is on the gig too.

Rhythmic inaccuracy is different from playing with a "feel," which may result in being intentionally ahead of or behind the beat. This gets into territory that's a little difficult to quantify because many traditional and pop styles have a "feel" that is not rhythmically precise, and in fact, it is that very imprecision which defines the style. I'm thinking of the way the second 16th note is pushed by traditional samba groups in Brazil, or the way rappers will lag way behind the beat, even when they are articulating the Groovon with the vocal. Or, a traditional Viennese waltz, which has a bit of a lopsided feel.

> **Feel**
>
> The personality that you bring to a groove; those subtle intangibles of timing and dynamics that create a rhythmic character.

It's OK, You're Improvising

When you apply the idea of placekeeper notes to melodies and phrases, you will be adding your own notes to those that are written on the page. It's OK! Assume that the notes on the page are there to guide you, not constrain you. Yes, technically you are improvising rhythmically. But don't panic! All you are doing is filling in the rhythm. You are adding rhythmic placekeeper notes.

Filling in the Melody

In the following exercises, we will practice filling in any note longer than a sixteenth note—the Groovon—with ghosted Groovons. While you probably won't want to perform a melody this way, it's useful to learn how to apply the concept of subdivision to melodies.

Here is a traditional melody in its original state:

Ex. 5A

And here is the placekeeper version with the placekeeper notes shown as ghost notes:

Ex. 5B

Rhythmic Integrity: The Placekeeper Workout

The concept of continuous strumming may help retain the rhythmic integrity of a melody by prompting you to change your bowing choices. Here's an example in 6/8 time to show how this approach can be applied to a different meter. Many string players might bow this phrase with as-it-comes bowing:

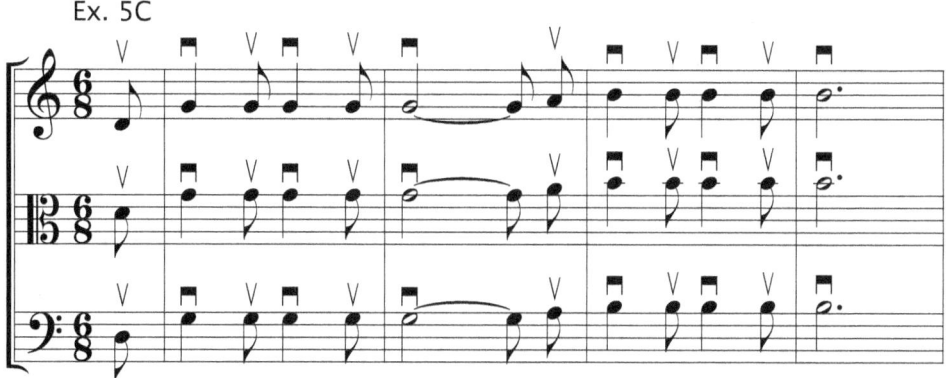

As I discussed in "An Introduction to Strum Bowing," the natural physics of the arm will make the uneven triplet figure tend towards two even dotted eighth notes.

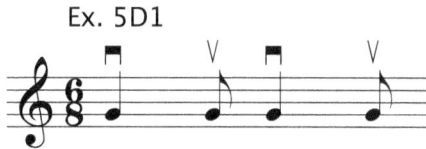

Turns into

Let's cure this lazy rhythm with a quick placekeeper work-out. First, we'll fill in the missing Groovons with ghost notes.

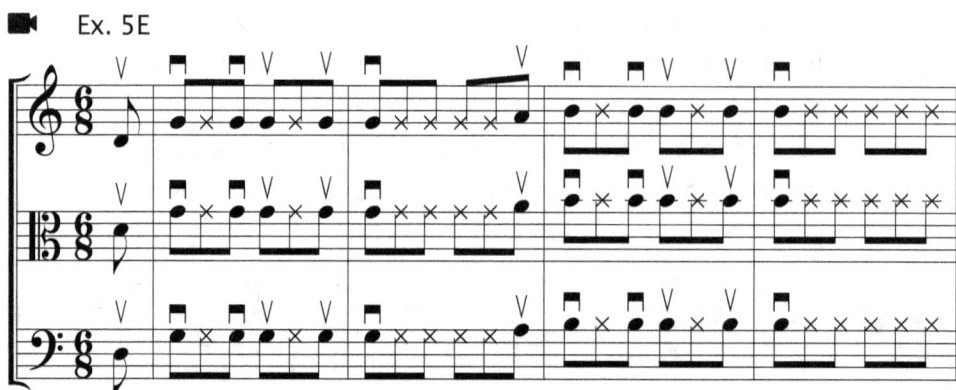

Sloppy rhythm is like bad muscle tone. Placekeeper notes will keep your grooves in shape.

Now that we have our inner drummer playing, let's ghost those placekeepers completely and remove them from the music while retaining the bowing they created. When you play this next example, the key is to still feel those missing placekeepers in your bow arm. Think them more than play them. It's as if you're ghosting them so completely that you're not even moving your arm. But, you're still clearly hearing them played by your inner drummer. Notice how the rhythm may be more accurate with this bowing? The physics are working with you instead of against you.

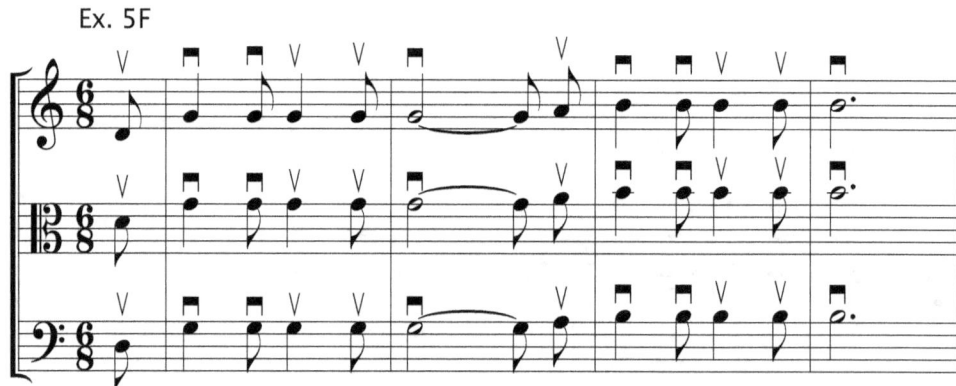

I've used the two previous melodies because they are so familiar, making it easier to understand the concept. But here is an example from a jazz tune where ghosting is actually stylistically appropriate. This is a tune by Sonny Rollins called "Pent Up House."

If we play it with as-it-comes bowing, it will look like this:

Let's fill in the placekeeper notes with ghosts:

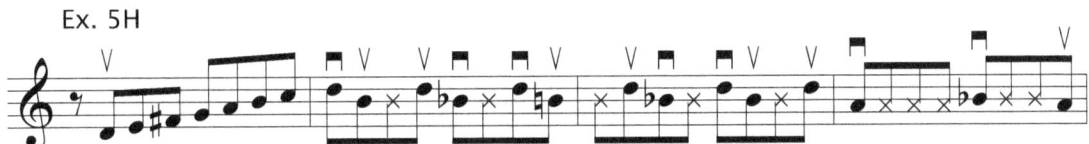

If we remove the placekeeper notes from the written music but continue to ghost them anyway, retaining the bowing as if we were playing all the Groovons, we are left with this bowing, which I refer to as the Bowing Key derived from Strum Bowing. It should make this melody more rhythmically accurate than with the as-it-comes bowing, and the slightly audible ghost notes add a jazzy feel:

It's a musical decision as to where or to what extent you want to use the bowing patterns derived from Strum Bowing. It's often a matter of how much of the rhythmic or dance-like character you want to bring to a melodic line. Strum Bowing enables you to choose a bowing that supports the rhythmic integrity of not only groove-based music but classical music as well. (See Chapter 20: "The Rhythm of Melody—Bringing Strum Bowing into Classical Playing.")

Bowing Key

The bow directions determined by Strum Bowing; the bowing that results when you add placekeeper notes to a phrase and impose a constant down/up bowing grid, then remove the placekeepers but retain the bowing.

Placekeeper Notes

March to the beat of your inner drummer.

How Do I Know What The Bowing Should Be?

One of the big challenges of playing grooves on strings is to figure out a bowing that will lend itself to the most authentic groove. Strum Bowing makes this very simple because it always adheres to the constant down/up grid. Any accents landing on a downbeat will be a down bow, and accents on up beats will be up bows. It's important to remember that down beats and up beats are determined by the Groovon value. For instance, if the Groovon is the sixteenth note, all the odd numbered sixteenths are down bows, and all the even numbered sixteenths are up bows.

Play
Fill in the Blanks

You can apply placekeeper notes to any melody. Choose a classical piece you know, and fill in all the held notes—any notes longer than the Groovon value, usually a sixteenth note—with placekeeper notes. Try a few classical melodies in different tempos and meters. Then, try this with melodies from non-classical styles.

March to the beat of your inner drummer.

Placekeeper Notes

The Lyrical, Rhythmical Life of the Irish Bow

TRADITIONALLY IN IRISH MUSIC, there weren't many accompaniment or percussion instruments to provide rhythm for dancers. The bow became a percussion tool that many fiddlers used in their own personal ways to create rhythm for the dance. I spent many of my formative years in a band playing for dancers. It was here that I began to get the pulse of this music into my body. Since then, I've been learning how to fully express this swing through the bow. Though I mostly perform in concert situations these days, I still use rhythmic bowing to produce a rhythm and pulse that supports the melodic ideas that I wish to express.

A beautiful and soulful melody can often be more easily expressed from your heart when resting on the hypnosis of a rhythm. Rhythm in itself can also induce an emotional response while also acting on a primal level to bring us into deeper contact with our bodies.

The bow is the source of lyrical expression for the fiddle and is also the source of pulse, They don't have to be mutually exclusive. I've spent a good part of my musical life trying to be simultaneously lyrical and rhythmic.

When I heard Tracy was going to write about his strum bowing I was immediately interested because the rhythm of the bow has been an integral part of my musical journey. Getting another perspective in this neglected area is a very valuable thing, especially when it comes from someone like Tracy who has carved out such a unique approach to the fiddle.

Martin Hayes
Irish fiddler
(The Gloaming, The Martin Hayes Quartet)

6. If You Can Say It, You Can Play It
The Power of Vocalizing

See: Groove Study 7

You can vastly speed up your learning process just by using your voice. The act of speaking or singing is deeply integrated into the learning process: in order to speak clearly, you have to think clearly.

Thoughts can sometimes be blissfully vague: they can breeze over details and happily ignore grey areas. But when you speak or sing out loud, you force yourself to commit to specific words or pitches. When you learn something new, whether it's a fiddle tune, a groove or Spanish vocabulary, saying it out loud will help you learn it faster because it forces you to be conscious of the details.

We go through a lot of life without thinking about every detail. We use a kind of autopilot called muscle memory all the time. In fact, we probably couldn't even walk or talk if we had to be aware of every little part of the process. We're fluent in our main language because we don't have to think about each verb conjugation, and we can walk up a flight of stairs because we learned how to do that a long time ago—we don't have to remind ourselves which foot comes next.

> **If You Can Say It, You Can Play It**
>
> Your larynx is located between your brain and your arms. When you say things out loud, your voice makes the connection between your brain and fingers. Coincidence? I don't think so.

Talk to the Hand

If it's a new pattern or groove you're after, you can't rely on muscle memory. You're trying to create new muscle memory, so you need to tell your arm and hands exactly what you want them to do.

Your bow arm is happy to do what it's told, but it needs a clear command first. If you sing a groove and tell your bow arm to play the accents you sing, that is pretty specific info, and it helps a lot in the process of coordinating your bow with the groove. But you can be even more specific with your mental commands so that there's no possibility of confusion by speaking the bow directions out loud. "Down up down" is more specific than "Dah dah dah." Your arm may be very skilled, but don't assume it's smart. Give it clear instructions.

In order to ensure an open flow of precise communication from your brain's command center to your obedient arms and hands, it helps to say the instructions out loud instead of just thinking them in your head. Otherwise, the muscle memory in your hands will be happy to go back to autopilot.

Your arm may be very skilled, but don't assume it's smart. Give it clear instructions.

The Voice Knows

Saying things out loud always shows you what you don't really know. You can't fake it if you have to name every note or bow direction. Vocalizing forces you to be fully conscious.

When there is something I can't quite get in a piece, I have learned it's usually because I'm not thinking it all the way through—there is some little place in the music where I'm not quite connecting the dots. There's a gap in my understanding somewhere. Any gap in the stream of instructions you send to your bow arm creates an opening for confusion.

Whenever you encounter some sort of stumbling block in music—or anything else—your first suspicion should be a gap in

> *In order to speak clearly, you have to think clearly.*

your understanding, some little spot where you think it's one thing but it's actually something else. Often, the problem is as simple as thinking a stroke is an up bow when in fact it's a down bow. When you break it down slowly, you realize the error. You find that you hadn't actually thought it through completely. Part of you, the part that loves being blissfully vague, was simply guessing and hoping. Miles Davis wasn't guessing. Bach wasn't hoping. Those guys knew exactly what they were doing.

My teacher, Debbra Wood Schwartz, used to say, "Playing the violin is hard enough. You don't need to add confusion."

I remember when I was young, I tried to define a word for my father. I couldn't quite verbalize what the word meant and said, "Well, I know what it means, I just can't explain it."

He said, "If you really knew exactly what it meant, you would have no trouble explaining it. The only reason you can't explain it is because you don't have a truly clear understanding of it." As annoying as that was to hear, it was true.

> *"Playing the violin is hard enough. You don't need to add confusion."*
> - Debbra Wood Schwartz

For instance, I may think, "I want the melody I improvise to go something like this." My arms gesture a general rise and fall of the line while I sort of hum a few indistinct notes in no particular key. If I try to play that solo, I will probably stumble at some point or possibly wander into the wrong key. But if I think, "the melody I'm hearing in my head goes exactly like this" and clearly sing the notes on pitch—and even better, say the names of the notes as I sing them—I will have a much greater chance of playing it right. The more specific I am, the better the chance I have of nailing it.

Even if there are no gaps and you are conscious of all the details, the act of singing or saying them out loud will help you remember them better than just thinking silently would.

Speak With Your Bow

Saying things out loud not only forces you to give clear, unambiguous instructions, it also helps your hands play the instrument. This is because we naturally tend to link our hands with our voice. Just watch how people gesticulate with their hands in order to make a point while speaking. Why not put that to good use? When you sing a rhythm, it makes it easier to play if the accents in your voice match the accents in your arm. Just try to sing one rhythm and play another and you'll see what I mean. Your voice naturally reinforces the physical motion.

Your Inner Voice

My definition of improvisation is to play on your instrument what you hear in your head. That means that you have to hear something in your head first.

In order to sing a tone, you must first hear that tone in your head. That's called audiation. It's virtually impossible to sing a tone without hearing it in your head beforehand. As with the voice, there are no keys, no buttons and no frets on string instruments. If you can't hear a note beforehand, you can't play it in tune.

A good way to apply this power of your voice is to simply sing along as you improvise. It seems very difficult to do, but it's actually easier than you might think. It's like thinking about what you want to say just before you say it, rather than blurting something out and possibly regretting it later.

If you say it (or sing it), it will be clearer in your mind and easier to play it. It's one of the most effective ways to maximize your practice or study time because it forces you to think clearly. And as far as I have been able to tell, clear thinking and clear intention are the keys to greatness in any field, from sports to academics to the arts.

My definition of improvisation is to play on your instrument what you hear in your head.

As far as I have been able to tell, clear thinking and clear intention are the keys to greatness in any field, from sports to academics to the arts.

Thinking as a (Black) Violinist: Investment, Precision and Boundless Imagination

I AM A BLACK VIOLINIST, but you don't have to be Black to think or play like me. Race has nothing to do with it. Rather, race is just another way to think about how you can approach your instrument. Consider yourself an actor, where you can approach, appropriate, and aspire to the music you've always wanted (and needed!) to make.

INVESTMENT/Margate, 1976

For me, my race and culture has been an important tool that I've incorporated into my playing. As a Black, Haitian-American violinist, I started playing the violin when I was 6 years old in Margate, Florida. And it's not that I just started to play the violin. I really wanted to play the violin. It was a deep, urgent, vital need to play. There was never a question about it. I fell in love with the look, feel, and sound of it all. The violin chose me!

In 1976, Margate didn't have many Black people or a Haitian community. I had no models. There was no way for me to see what I felt everyday, namely, a Black, Haitian violinist.

And it didn't matter. I decided to invest in the violin at great cost to me at that time. It was an investment that I wanted and needed, but one that isolated me from my friends, and oftentimes made me feel like "the other". Beyond race and culture, most musicians I know have been made to feel this way at some point in our lives. It hurts. But know, you're making a life-long investment and it will be worth it more than any of us can possibly know or understand.

PRECISION/Dance to it!

From the blues, to rock music, to Rihanna, we are surrounded by Black music. It's important that as we consider groove, we consider and be precise about the kind of groove music you're studying, listening to, and aspiring to make. By simply listening to a broad spectrum of Black music, you will deepen your understanding of how music can have complex, interlocking, rhythmic nuances, that all form a singular groove.

Listen to Black music by Black musicians. Move to it! Dance to it! Sing it! Embody it! The most fundamental aspects of learning to play groove music, begins by learning to listen to groove music. Be precise in your choices, and Black music is a very good place to start.

IMAGINATION/Sade Pizz.

After you've invested and committed to your instrument, and as you sharpen your listening choices, it will be important for you to know your imagination is the most important skill you will always have as a part of your musical technique. How you apply your imagination to your music making is a life-long conversation you should have with your instrument, teachers, friends, family, and community, as you develop more ways to make different types of music.

Allow me to offer an example. I was taught there were only two, essential pizzicatos: a standard pizzicato and the Bartok pizzicato. This is not true, and there are dozens of ways to pluck the strings and create new tones and sounds.

Using the nail of your index finger, pluck the string repeatedly as close to the bridge as possible. Try to create an electric, metallic sound. Use as much pressure as possible, then, the least amount. Vary the amount, continuously, as you pluck the string repeatedly. I refer to this as a "sul ponticello pizzicato", or, my "Sade Pizz", named for the Nigerian and British soul singer, Sade Adu. I have dozens of different ways in which I approach pizzicato on my violin, many of which are responses to the sounds made by my favorite blues, rock, and soul musicians.

As you invest in what you want to do with your music, be precise in your choices and approaches, and allow your boundless imagination to inform and infuse the music you want and need to make.

Daniel Bernard Roumain (DBR)
Professor of Practice & Institute Professor
Herberger Institute for Design and the Arts (ASU)
www.danielroumain.com

7. The Dance of the Groove
The Power of Physicalizing

See: Groove Study 8

> **Physicalize**
>
> To actualize your inner drummer, i.e. to express the subdivision physically as a strum or other motion; to allow your body to respond to a groove with movement; to dance to the groove.

Bodies in Motion

Good rhythm playing is always accompanied by some kind of rhythmic body movement: the "dance" of the groove. That's because, in a deeper sense, the musical groove is actually generated by this dance, this rhythmic way of moving your body and your bow. Rhythmic music is a by-product of rhythmic movement.

When you are connected to that sense of dance and allow it to guide the way you play, listeners respond in turn by dancing, or at least by feeling like they want to move. When dance inspires music, that music inspires dance. It's a non-vicious cycle.

When I use the term physicalize, I mean to unlock your muscles and allow your body to engage freely. That doesn't mean every muscle has to be swinging and swaying and rocking to the rhythm. It doesn't mean you have to move around and "perform" or put on a show. It means that you may be tapping your foot, nodding your head, twisting your hips or bouncing to the beat—whatever feels right to you. It means your body is free and allowed to move the way it's supposed to.

Rhythmic music is a by-product of rhythmic movement.

Not only does it feel good to physicalize, it's really the only way to keep a groove steady. Just ask a drummer or watch a rhythm guitar player. They're movin' to the groovin'. Isaac Newton's law of inertia states that "a body in motion stays in motion." Rhythm players are just letting the natural law of inertia help them. If you lock up your muscles and keep yourself from moving freely, you are depriving yourself of the most helpful tool you have to play grooves—your body. You are trying to defy the laws of physics. Good luck with that.

If, somewhere in your classical past, someone told you to stand still and stop moving, you need to try to forget that ever happened. Let your body help you.

Keep in mind, feeling free to move is not the same thing as jumping around or being randomly active while you're playing. It's very possible to get your body to move in ways that have nothing to do with the groove of the music. This non-musical movement usually looks and feels kind of awkward because it is awkward. If your movement isn't initiated by the rhythm of the groove, it won't be organic to the music. It will be superimposed onto the groove.

If you find yourself moving awkwardly, don't despair! There are only 2 reasons why this may occur: 1) your body is rigid and not free, or 2) you aren't really listening to the pulse and groove of the music. Or both. There are many good reasons why this may happen—nervousness, inhibitions, etc. But luckily, the solution is easy and fun.

When dance inspires music, that music inspires dance.

Getting into the Groove

First of all, don't try to move in rhythm. Let the rhythm move you instead. It may help to picture yourself as a guitar player or drummer and to remember that rhythm players always move in ways that help them play. Focus on the pulse and the groove until it makes you want to move, and then allow yourself to move. That's the tricky part for some people. But you know the refrain: if guitar players can do it, how hard can it be?

When I find myself tensing up and losing my "flow," I always think to myself, "Loosen up your knees. Relax and let the rhythm take over." The groove starts in your feet and works its way up to your bow arm.

Human-sized Time

The whole function of the strum is to keep time. When you physicalize the groove, your body becomes the metronome. As we learned in Chapter 2 ("The Grid—The Structure of Grooves."), the slower a pulse gets, the harder it gets to keep time evenly. A strong pulse once every minute is hard for us to define, but if we take that span of time and divide it into pulses every second, it becomes human-sized. We can't dance to a pulse once every minute, but we can dance to a pulse once every second.

In fact, we can physicalize that pulse in such a way that we can simultaneously subdivide it and make it even more accurate and steady. Try this: step back and forth in place on quarter notes, and while you nod your head up and down on eighth notes, strum your hand on sixteenth notes. It sounds complicated, but it should actually feel pretty natural. If it doesn't feel natural right away, just relax and play around with it for a while until it does.

All of these timekeepers not only help you define the accents and style of the groove, they also ensure that the groove will be consistent, solid and unwavering. Once you get your body in motion, it wants to stay in that motion, and the law of inertia keeps it steady. Without that steady motion, it's likely to rush or drag.

Grooves are born out of the rhythm of our heartbeat and breath. An uneven groove is like an irregular pulse. It makes us uncomfortable. Maybe the appeal of a groove is that it makes us feel like our heartbeat will never end, that our breathing will never stop. The steadiness of a groove is a metaphor for the continuity of life itself.

An inconsistent pulse is appropriate for rubato passages in classical music or "out of time" (with no steady beat) jazz ballads, but it's death to a groove. In the context of classical music, grooves may be interrupted or manipulated more than in

The groove starts in your feet and works its way up to your bow arm.

The steadiness of a groove is a metaphor for the continuity of life itself.

dance-based music. In classical music, having a groove doesn't mean there is never a ritard or a breath. But while that groove exists, it creates a sense of absolute steadiness.

A Groove is Forever

Even if you only hear one bar of it, a great groove creates the illusion of eternity. It could be an infectious James Brown groove that makes you feel that you could dance forever. Or the inexorable build of Ravel's Bolero. Or the sense that you've just come face to face with mother nature and father time in Bach's Chaconne or Beethoven's Ninth Symphony.

A great groove sounds like it has always been there, like it started before time began and will never end. Grooves represent infinity.

Grooves represent infinity.

A groove is like a million ton freight train on a flat prairie that's been rolling along at the exact same speed for days. You can't alter it. You just hop on and ride it for a while.

Play
Movin' and Groovin'

Make sure no one can see you. Choose some of your favorite music with a groove, and crank it up. Listen carefully to all the different rhythmic elements that may be at work. Let your body respond to them—first your feet and legs, then your core and finally your arms and head. Pay attention to which parts of your body seem to react to which parts of the groove. Then, pick another piece of music and try it again. Repeat.

Bow Circles

HERE'S A RHYTHMIC BOWING TECHNIQUE that's common across all traditional fiddling styles, but especially used in Appalachian old-time and Celtic fiddling. It uses the same principle as Strum bowing, and gets the job done for groove in melodies. It's also very effective for swingy and jazz styles.

We'll start with upbeat, or offbeat notes. Put your bow on the string at about 3/4 or 7/8 of the way toward the tip. Then make small clockwise circles (about 3-4 inches in diameter) with your right hand, holding the bow normally. You'll notice that the bow digs into the string lightly on the bottom of the circle and floats off the string a bit on the top arc, giving a ghost note effect.

If we do the same thing but reverse the direction of the circle to counter-clockwise, we once again get a more solid bow contact on the bottom of the circle, and a breathy effect on the top of the arc.

Again, if we think of the downbow arc of the circle as being on the downbeat and the upbow part as being on the offbeat, we get a nice breathy rhythmic sound with not much effort and plenty of groove feeling. The circular motion smooths out the stroke and reduces the amount of energy needed for fast rhythms. Often in Southern Appalachian fiddling, the high-speed interaction of melody and string crossings create an intricate and hypnotic combination of circular and figure-8 strokes, which would be difficult to sustain for more than a few seconds without this smoothing-out action.

Darol Anger
Founding member, Turtle Island String Quartet
Assoc. Prof., Berklee College of Music
www.darolanger.com

8. GPS: Groove Proficiency System
Practice Groove 1

See: Groove Study 9

> **GPS (Groove Proficiency System) for Strings**
>
> 1. **Hum It** Get It in Your Voice: Vocalize the Groove
> 2. **Strum It** Get It in Your Body: Find the Groovon
> 3. **Say It** Get It in Your Brain: Discover the Bow Direction
> 4. **Play It!** Get It on Your Instrument

Grooves are very physical things. They may not always feel natural at first because you need to develop new muscle memory. You may have to overwrite some previous muscle memory that is keeping you from hitting the accents you intend to bring out. Or, there may be a gap in your understanding. Somehow you may have gotten it in your head one way when it's actually something slightly different. (See Ch. 6: "If You Can Say It, You Can Play It—The Power of Vocalizing.")

This is when it helps to let your voice clear up your thinking. It's time to break it down and connect the dots with your voice-activated Grove Proficiency System. It's GPS for Strings!

GPS for Strings
The Secret to Learning New Grooves

The process for learning new grooves is very simple. The idea is "If you can say it, you can play it." Here's how that actually breaks down: **get it in your voice, get it in your body, get it in your brain, and get it on your instrument.**

The GPS for Strings is effective because you first learn the groove viscerally through physical and verbal repetition, and then you activate your intellect with specific bow directions. If you follow these four steps, there is no groove you cannot learn.

We've actually already used the GPS in Chapter 3 ("Strum 101—Getting Your Groovon."), but let's figure out what we did so we can use it to learn new grooves.

1. Hum It
Get It in Your Voice: Vocalize the Groove

Let's assume there is a recording of a groove that you want to learn. The first step in the process is to hear the groove, to be fully aware of it. Before you can play it, you have to know what it is you're trying to play. If you have an app that will loop and slow down a small section of a song such as the Amazing Slow Downer, use it to isolate the riff so you can easily repeat it and study it. We're going to use our voice to hear better because, as we learned in Chapter 6, when you activate your voice, you force your brain to be specific and aware of details.

When I say "Hum it," what I really mean is to sing the rhythm. Articulate all the down beats, all the accents, and if you can, all the little ghosted Groovons in between. You should end up sounding like you're beatboxing.

It's much more challenging to do this with a written rhythm than with a recording to imitate, but let's try. Put down your instrument for a moment and vocalize/beatbox this groove in Ex. 8A. It's the same one we've been working on. Allow your body to move freely and help you get into the groove. Go ahead and turn it into a whole drum kit or electronic drum beat in your imagination, complete with even the ghosted Groovons that are not indicated on the page.

Ex. 8A
Vocal only

Dah   dah   dah   dah   dah   dah dah

2. Strum It
Get It in Your Body: Find the Groovon

Have you ever had the experience of trying to play an up bow and a down bow at the same time?

Next, find the Groovon by imitating a shaker or air strumming an imaginary guitar. (See Ch. 1: "The Groovon—The Smallest Particle of the Groove.") As usual, it's the sixteenth note. Physicalize the Groovon by strumming in the air. Now pick up your bow, and keeping the same strumming motion, transition from air strumming a guitar to air bowing a string instrument. You should be air bowing all of the sixteenth notes, not just the accents, as if you are strumming with your bow. Keep beatboxing! That's your guide.

Ex. 8B

Dah   dah dah   dah   dah   dah dah

3. Say It
Get It in Your Brain: Discover the Bow Direction

This is where we use our voice to move from a more visceral awareness of the groove to a cerebral understanding of the specific bow directions.

Have you ever had the experience of trying to play something a little complicated, maybe a groove rhythm, and suddenly finding that you were trying to play an up bow and a down bow at the same time? Your bow arm ends up in a kind of paralysis or making tiny circular motions, while your brain sort of stutters and can't figure out what's going on. This is exactly what happens when there is a gap in your understanding.

This is why we need to get the bowing clear in our brain in order to play it.

Gradually slow down your beatboxing of the groove until you are going slowly enough to be able to verbalize the grid, and say the bow direction, "Down, up, down, up…" on each Groovon. Do this out loud, not in your head. You'd be surprised how often I have to remind people that "out loud" means a voice that other people can hear.

As you are saying "Down, up, down, up…" use both your air bowing and your voice to emphasize the accents of the groove. It should sound like this: "DOWN up down UP DOWN up down UP down UP down UP DOWN up down up."

The emphasized words are the bow directions of all the accents in the groove. Now drop all the unstressed notes, and what you're left with is the bow directions of all the accents. This is your bow direction key to playing the groove. "DOWN, UP DOWN, UP, UP, UP DOWN."

As we discovered in Chapter 6, we often gesture with our hands when we speak to emphasize important points, and it's very natural for us to connect our bow arm with the emphasis in our voice. These bow directions will help give clear, specific commands to your arm so that when you're ready to play, you'll know which notes to ghost and which to accentuate without losing the consistent up/down bow motion of the strum.

You'd be surprised how often I have to remind people that "out loud" means a voice that other people can hear.

Ex. 8C

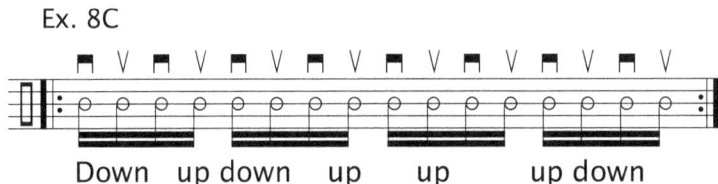

Down up down   up   up   up down

GPS: Groove Proficiency System   65

4. Play It!
Get It on Your Instrument

If you can say it, you can play it.

Keep saying the bow direction. In fact, feel free to shout these out like commands to your bow arm. It's important in this next step not to lose your flow, so keep air bowing to make sure you have your strum locked in.

Now, while you're still shouting those bow directions, go ahead and put your bow on the strings.

Keep the strum going the whole time while you emphasize the accents. Your bow will want to follow the emphasis of your voice, which is helpful. But because that voice/arm connection is so strong, it's entirely possible that your pre-Strum Bowing instincts may kick in, and you may regress to playing only the accents with as-it-comes bowing, leaving out all the ghosts in the strum. This is why we get a running start by air bowing first, in order to get that constant strum motion established.

At first, you may have too much droning going on with all the Groovons being played too loud, and you may have to dial in your ghosting. Remember to use tiny bows and little "pinches" on the accents. (See Ch. 4: "Ghost Notes—How to *Not* Play An Instrument.")

Ex. 8D

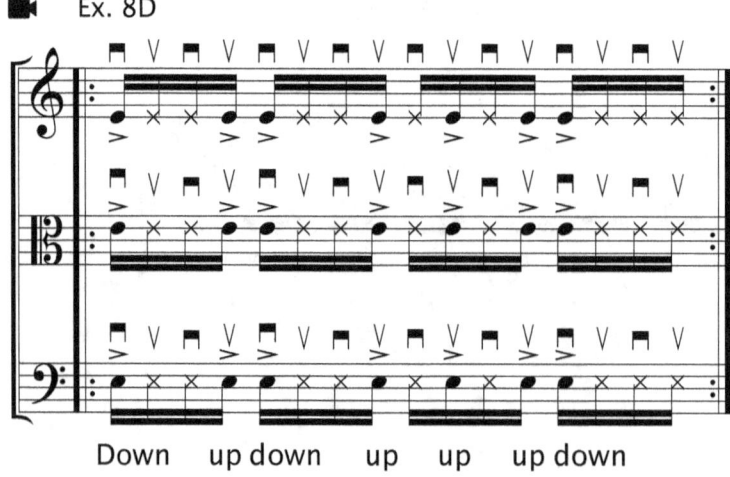

Compare and Contrast

Once you get the basic groove under control—once you have a steady stream of up/down bows with accents where they belong and ghosted Groovons that are not distracting—then you can shift your voice from shouting the bow directions back to your original vocalization of the groove.

Stop playing for a moment. Get your beatbox going as you did in step one. Then play your newly learned groove on the instrument.

Stop playing again, and listen carefully as you vocalize again. Then, start playing again and listen carefully to what you're playing. How are they different? (See "The Yin/Yang of Listening" in Ch. 10: "GPS: Groove Proficiency System—Practice Groove 3.") The goal is to try to make the sounds you play on your instrument as close as possible to the sounds you make with your voice. Don't add extra notes that you're not verbalizing, and don't leave out notes that you're emphasizing with your voice. If you can, try to beatbox and play at the same time.

The idea is to imitate your voice with your instrument: voice first, instrument second.

Don't worry if your playing isn't matching up exactly with your vocalizing yet. There is a wide palette of percussive sounds that we will soon have in our control and lots of open groove space to color in.

The idea is to imitate your voice with your instrument: voice first, instrument second.

Gesture Bowing

We use hand gestures for emphasis all the time. For instance, if I say, "I will never give up!" I might pound my fist on the word "Never." When I say, "I love this song!" I might show it by emphasizing the word "love" with a hand on my heart.

You can do this with a musical phrase as well. Sing a line from a tune and find it's most emphatic notes. For instance, in "Yesterday" by the Beatles, the most important syllables to emphasize would be the very first "Yes-" of "Yesterday" and "far" from the phrase, "All my troubles seemed so far away." (Incidentally, they are the downbeats of the first and third bars of the phrase.)

If you think about it, many downward hand gestures in speech actually resemble down bows. Sing "Yesterday" and gesture with a downward motion of your arm on the emphasized notes as you sing it. It should be a very natural motion, since you are imitating our natural tendency to emphasize key moments within speech. If you were to play this on a string instrument, it would be most natural to use down bows on those notes since down bows have more weight than up bows. I call this **gesture bowing—placing down bows on emphatic points in a phrase.** This is a great way to figure out the most natural bow patterns for any style, and it's especially useful for complicated bebop jazz phrases.

The law of Strum Bowing dictates that all accented up beats—syncopations—should be played with an up bow, since the note lands on an up bow on the grid of continual down/up bows. This presents a conflict with the idea of gesture bowing, in which you would emphasize accents with down bows. My rule of thumb for syncopation is this: if a phrase is primarily melodic, use ges-

---

> **Gesture Bowing**
>
> Emphasizing with your bow arm the way you might if you were speaking emphatically.

ture bowing, emphasizing with down bows; if a phrase is primarily rhythmic, like a groove, use Strum Bowing, accenting with up bows. But, keep in mind that every rule has exceptions.

Play
Gesturing the Groove

You won't need your instrument for this one. Start with a groove from a song you like or one you've invented. Imitate the groove with your voice—beatbox the groove. Gesticulate with your hands while you beatbox. Allow your body to respond to the accents and power of the beat, and let it move as freely as it wants to. Pick another tune. Repeat.

9. GPS: Groove Proficiency System
Practice Groove 2

See: Groove Study 10

Let's learn a new groove using our GPS from the last chapter:

> **GPS (Groove Proficiency System) for Strings**
>
> 1. **Hum It**   Get It in Your Voice: Vocalize the Groove
> 2. **Strum It**   Get It in Your Body: Find the Groovon
> 3. **Say It**   Get It in Your Brain: Discover the Bow Direction
> 4. **Play It!**   Get It on Your Instrument

1. Hum It
Get It in Your Voice: Vocalize the Groove

Put down your instrument and beatbox this groove. As before, allow your body to move freely and help you get into the groove. You can make drum sounds, or you can say "Dah dah dah" or anything you like. You could say "Bar-Bar-Bar, Bar-be-cue Pork" because the groove sounds a little like "Barbara Ann" by the Beach Boys. (If you're a vegetarian, you can say "Bro-Bro-Bro, Broc-co-li Soup.")

Ex. 9A

2. Strum It
Get It in Your Body: Find the Groovon

While you beatbox, find the Groovon by imitating a shaker or air strumming an imaginary guitar. Pick up the bow, and keep the same motion, strumming all of the sixteenth notes with your bow.

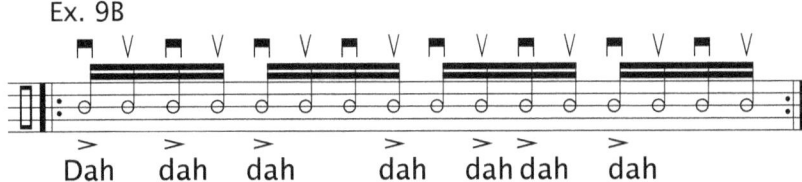

Ex. 9B

3. Say It
Get It in Your Brain: Discover the Bow Direction

Slow it down so you can verbalize the grid and say "Down, up, down, up…" on each Groovon, but maintain the accents from the groove as you do this. It should sound like this: "DOWN up DOWN up DOWN up down UP down UP DOWN up DOWN up down up." This reveals your lyric key to this groove as, "DOWN DOWN DOWN, UP, UP DOWN DOWN." These are the commands you need to give to your bow arm as you air bow.

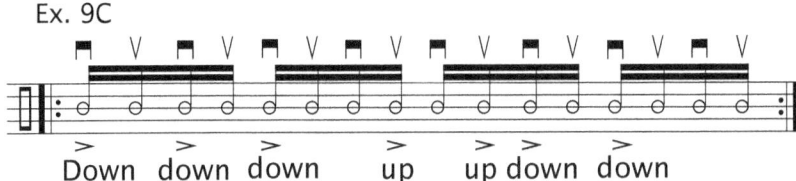

Ex. 9C

4. Play It!
Get It on Your Instrument

If you can say it, you can play it.

Keep saying the bow direction, and keep air bowing to make sure you have your strum locked in. Put your bow on the strings, and keep it moving in sixteenth notes while your voice helps you bring out the accents: "DOWN DOWN DOWN, UP, UP DOWN DOWN."

Ex. 9D

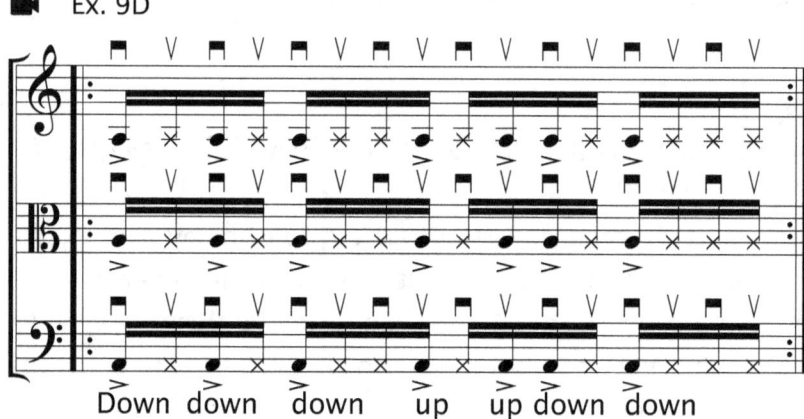

Try to get those ghosts to vanish into thin air. Remember to use tiny bows!

Stop and go back to beatboxing the groove. Compare your instrumental groove to your beatbox version. Try to imitate your voice.

Play
Compare Strum Bowing with As-It-Comes Bowing.

Try playing the groove from this chapter with as-it-comes bowing like this:

Ex. 9E

Is it harder to play the rhythm accurately this way? Try it faster and check your precision with a metronome.

Now, go back to the Strum Bowing version:

Ex. 9F

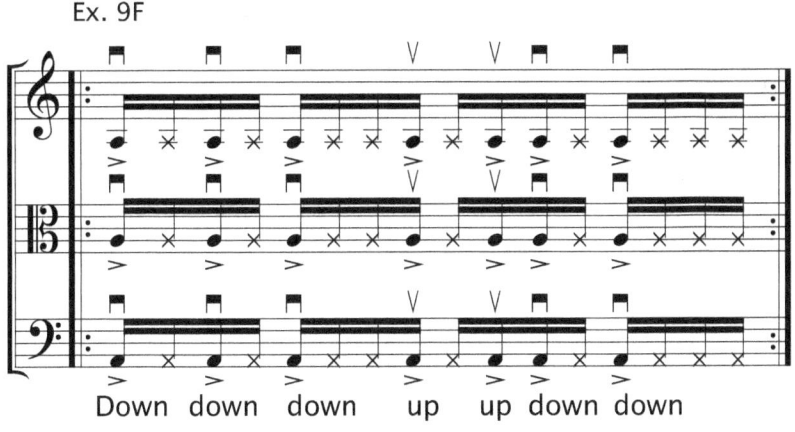

Which way seems steadier?

Finding the Funk

FOR ME, LEARNING TO GROOVE as a violinist came from years of leading a double life outside of my classical studies, playing guitar and bass in rock and funk bands. One of the most important things I learned was the importance of locking in with a drummer. Most classically trained string players never get the opportunity to learn this skill.

I remember spending countless hours in my room playing bass or guitar along with my favorite tracks, be it Kiss, Led Zeppelin, James Brown, or Miles Davis. The goal was to try to emulate the bass or rhythm guitar and lock in perfectly with the drums. Players who could do this the best possessed the "pocket," and I was trying to chase the perfect pocket for many years.

For string players, I would highly recommend actually learning bass or guitar and putting yourself in a situation where you have to play as part of a good rhythm section.

But as far as your own instrument is concerned, here are a few suggestions:
- Take any funk or pop song, transcribe or learn the rhythm guitar part by ear. Play that pattern by itself, bowing "as it comes."
- Next, try playing all the sixteenth notes and focusing on the rhythmic pattern you just learned, while "ghosting" the less important notes.

A good example of this is the rhythm guitar part for the song "Uptown Funk" by Bruno Mars and Mark Ronson.

Here is the basic guitar pattern:

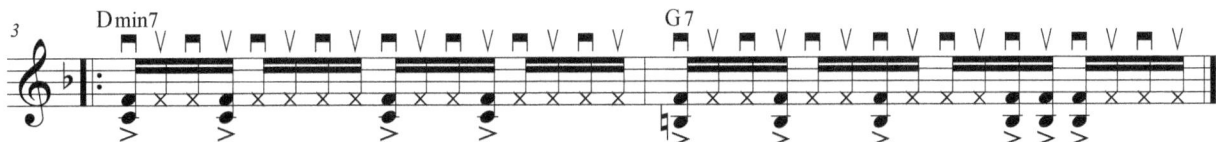

"Ghost" the 16ths in between the accents: play them quietly, or mute them with the pinky of your left hand. The tempo of the song is around 114 bpm, but I would recommend you start at about 80 and work your way up.

Once you are comfortable playing this simple rhythmic pattern with the strumming/muting, I recommend isolating as many different rhythm guitar patterns of funk songs as you can, practicing the same approach with each.

Finally, try to get yourself into as many real-life playing situations as possible, whether it's a gig, jam session, or just playing with friends. Try to come up with your own "strumming," rhythm guitar parts to songs. Go against your instinct and aim to assume the role of the rhythm guitar in the band, not the traditional melodic role of your instrument. If there is another guitarist playing a syncopated pattern, try to come up with your own pattern that compliments what the guitarist is playing and doesn't get in the way. Some of the best funk songs of all time had multiple instruments playing different syncopations that locked in and grooved hard! Just because you're a string player, don't ever let anyone tell you that you can't bring the funk!

Best of luck! Stay in the pocket and get your GROOVON!

Joe Deninzon,

Electric Violinist, (Stratospheerius)

www.joedeninzon.com

Finding the Funk

10. GPS: Groove Proficiency System
Practice Groove 3

See: Groove Study 11

Maybe by this point you're thinking to yourself, "This is a lot of trouble. My rhythm isn't that bad. I think I'm going to skip ahead to the Chop section."

If that's you, here's another little demonstration of why Strum Bowing is useful to even the most highly-trained players.

First, play the following riff with as-it-comes bowing. Here's an example of how most players would approach this phrase:

Ex. 10A

Does it really groove well that way? This bowing doesn't adhere well to a grid because it's hard to start and stop the bow accurately. (See "An Introduction to Strum Bowing.") Even if you can play it accurately, it may still sound stiff or stylistically unconvincing. That's in large part because it's missing all the little ghosted Groovons that we're used to hearing in this style.

It's steadier and stylistically more correct to find and physicalize the subdivision (the Groovon) with a strumming motion and fill the spaces between the notes with ghost notes. When we do that, we discover that the bowing for this riff works out to be this:

Ex. 10B

The bowing may look odd and non-intuitive, and if you lift and retake the repeated down and up bows in a more traditional manner, it will sound odd too. Example 10B is the shorthand notation, the map view. The satellite view, what you actually play, looks like this:

Ex. 10C

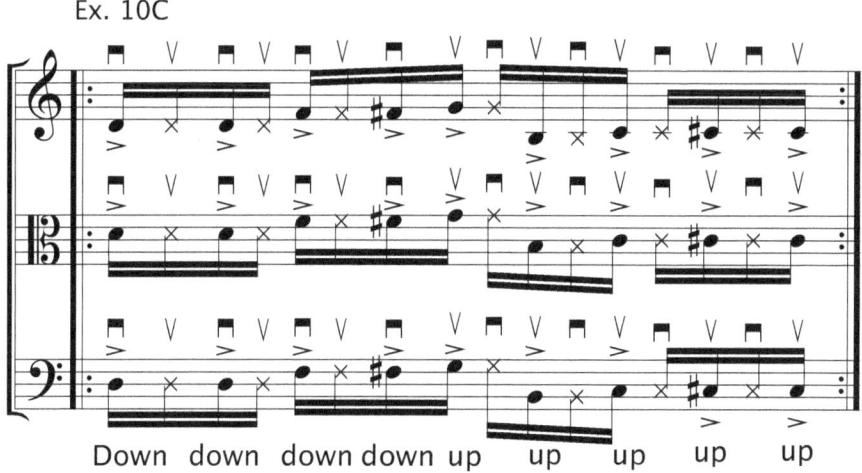

Down down down down up   up   up   up   up

Let's break it down using the GPS for Strings from Chapter 8.

> **GPS (Groove Proficiency System) for Strings**
>
> 1. **Hum It** Get It in Your Voice: Vocalize the Groove
> 2. **Strum It** Get It in Your Body: Find the Groovon
> 3. **Say It** Get It in Your Brain: Discover the Bow Direction
> 4. **Play It!** Get It on Your Instrument

1. Hum It
Get It in Your Voice: Vocalize the Groove

Vocalize the groove in Ex. 10D below. This one has more of a melody, not just a rhythm, so you may need to go back and forth between singing the riff and singing the drum groove—that is, between a pitched and a non-pitched version of the riff. Our only goal is to internalize the rhythm. If you can say it, you can play it. Once you get it in your voice, you can physicalize it in preparation to better achieve it on your instrument. Go ahead and let your body move with the groove.

Ex. 10D

2. Strum It
Get It in Your Body: Find the Groovon

While you're vocalizing the rhythm, find the Groovon, the fastest moving part of the groove. Once again, it's the sixteenth note. Strum it in the air. Then, pick up the bow and air bow it. Remember, you're air bowing all the sixteenth notes, not only the accents. Keep singing that rhythm!

Ex. 10E

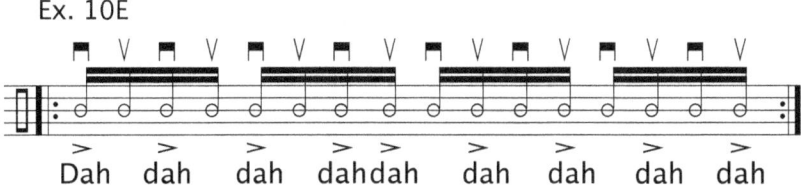

3. Say It
Get It in Your Brain: Discover the Bow Direction

Now, instead of vocalizing "Dah Dah" (or whatever nonsense syllable you prefer), call out the bow directions of the accents as you air bow. Give your arm specific directions (in both senses of the word).

If you need to, slow it down and say "Down up down up" for every sixteenth note while emphasizing the accents. It should sound like this: "DOWN up DOWN up DOWN up DOWN UP down UP down UP down UP down UP." Then, drop out the unstressed words to reveal your bow direction key: "DOWN DOWN DOWN DOWN UP UP UP UP."

Ex. 10F

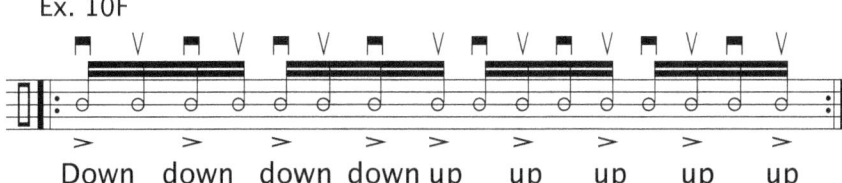

4. Play It!
Get It on Your Instrument

Now, place your bow on the string, play all of the sixteenth notes, and let your voice direct your arm to emphasize the accents of the groove. Try to ghost those placekeeper notes as much as possible. Remember to use tiny bow strokes and to mute the strings with your left hand when you play the ghost notes. Don't stop calling out the bow direction! Use your voice to make the connection between your brain and your hand, but don't let the vocal emphasis on the accents lure you into only bowing the accents. Make sure you keep strumming ghost notes on all the Groovons.

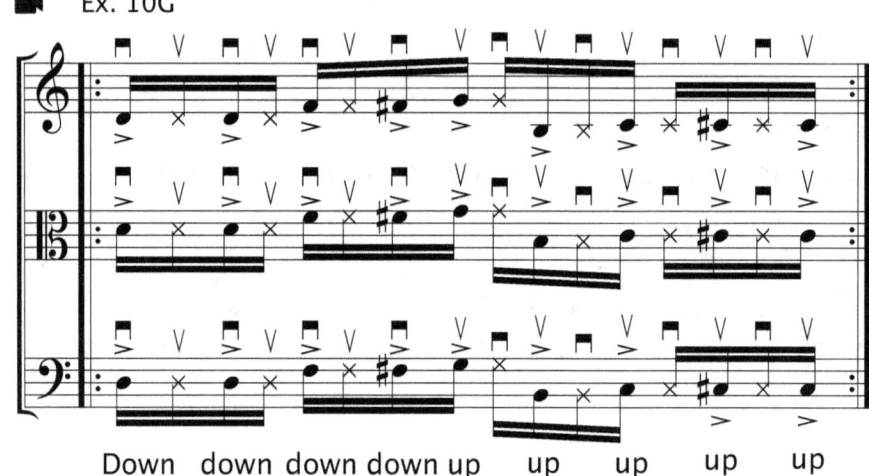

Ex. 10G

Down   down   down   down   up   up   up   up

Applying Strum Bowing to any riff is a simple process that never changes: all down beats are down bow and all up beats are up bow. Easy to remember.

Chapters 8 through 10 have demonstrated how you can apply Strum Bowing to any riff. It's a simple process that never changes: all down beats are down bow and all up beats are up bow. Easy to remember.

Now go back and try the as-it-comes, bowing the way you did at the beginning of this chapter in Ex. 10A. The traditional approach to playing this rhythm just doesn't cut it. To sound stylistically authentic, use this Strum Bowing version instead:

Ex.10H

The more vivid your imagination, the better your odds of recreating it.

The Yin/Yang of Listening

The listening process of a musician is different from the listening experience of the audience. A musician has to listen forward as well as backward.

On the one hand, you need to think ahead, to imagine a sound and to "hear" it as distinctly as if you are actually playing it. This is called audiation. It's the sound you shoot for: the ideal version of the pitch, tone or phrasing in your imagination that you try to match with your instrument. The more vivid your imagination, the better your odds of recreating it.

On the other hand, you have to be able to do the opposite kind of listening. This is the examination of the actual sound you are making, not the one you hoped you would make. This is not what you would sound like if you had a better instrument or a better amp, or a better night's sleep or a cup of coffee beforehand. This is not what you wish you sounded like. This is the actual sound coming out of your instrument: the reality check. Which notes are out of tune? Which notes stick out unintentionally? Which accents aren't really as pronounced as you'd like them to be? Is the groove really as perfectly in time as you imagine it to be? It's very useful to make quick audio or video recordings of your practice to check yourself.

My dad used to say, "Listen to yourself practice as if it was your brother playing."

As musicians, we are constantly situated within the dichotomy between the ideal sound in our head and the real sound on our instruments. We make instantaneous adjustments to pitch and tone all the time, trying to reshape our reality to match our ideal. When we split our attention equally between ideal and real, we can clearly hear what we're not yet achieving. Honest confrontations with shortcomings may not be as blissful as ignoring them, but paying attention to reality allows us to adjust as quickly as possible.

If we are able to achieve a balance between these two ways of listening—imagining the ideal while simultaneously assessing the real—we can make these adjustments with Jedi-like speed, precision and control.

That's the yin/yang of listening.

If we achieve a balance between imagining the ideal while assessing the real, we can make adjustments with Jedi-like speed, precision and control.

Play
Random Tunes

The best way to develop a well-rounded technique is to work in a number of different genres. Just as we are better people when we know and love many different kinds of people, we are better musicians when we know and love many different kinds of music.

Surf a variety of radio stations or Internet playlists, or choose tunes randomly from your music collection. Whatever tune comes up, challenge yourself to break down the learning process with the Groove Proficiency System and figure out how to play it using Strum Bowing.

The Groovon can reflect or influence the energy level as it changes throughout a song.

Play
Ghost Notes

This would be a good time to review your ghost note technique. Remember to use small bows. Play Ex. 10G over and over, and experiment with bow pressure and left hand dampening. Try to control the exact amount of sound produced by the ghost notes, from 100% down to 50%. Then, try to get them down to 25%, and finally, to zero. The goal is to match your ghosting response with your exact intention. There is no right or wrong amount to ghost. In fact, it's common for rhythm players to modify a groove constantly by varying the audibility of the ghost notes in response to other players or singers in a group. (See Ch. 11: "Variety is the Spice of Grooves—The Power of the Strum.") Just as the Groovon has great influence on the tempo and style (See Ch. 1: "The Groovon—The Smallest Particle of the Groove"), the Groovon can also reflect or influence the energy level as it changes throughout a song. That's why drum fills work so well: they bring energy to a phrase by exaggerating the Groovons.

This is why it's important to develop your mastery of the ghost note technique. Ghosting is at the heart of contemporary groove styles, but it is very new territory for many string players.

Practice Groove 3 is a good candidate for finger dampening, especially if you don't use an open string for the D note. For contrast, go back and revisit Ex. 9F from the previous chapter. That groove is well suited for pinky dampening. Experiment with all the interesting rhythmic sounds you can produce on those ghost notes. Feel free to mess around with the groove and let it morph into something else. Now that you've learned how to control it precisely, allow yourself to let it wander wherever it wants to go. Explore. Have fun. Be playful.

Just as we are better people when we know and love many different kinds of people, we are better musicians when we know and love many different kinds of music.

11. Variety is the Spice of Grooves
The Power of the Strum

See: Groove Study 12

Good rhythm playing is vibrantly alive and constantly in flux. It breathes with the music. The real power of Strum Bowing is that it encourages flexibility and rhythmic variation by focusing on the underlying concept of subdivision rather than learning individual rote patterns.

The Magic of the Up Beat

Have you ever heard live music that was just kind of dull? It felt like everyone was waiting for something good to happen, and the energy was just kind of dragging? Or the opposite, when the energy starts taking off, as if everyone is going to lift off the stage? What makes one groove boring and another infectious?

When music is effective, there are many things going right. While it's nearly impossible to put your finger on the magic of music, I have noticed something consistent and surprisingly simple: the magic usually has to do with up beat energy. By "up beat," I don't mean an upbeat mood, I mean the even-numbered subdivisions of the beat, the up bows of the strum. Not surprisingly, this has everything to do with the Groovon. When we subdivide a beat, we are creating up beats.

Great players get you to feel the subdivisions.

One of the factors leading to my groundbreaking discovery of the Groovon particle was noticing that great players get you to feel the subdivisions, either directly or implicitly, bringing out the fast, inner rhythmic energy that propels so much music. This way of playing comes from a deep, physical sense of the groove that allows your body to reflect the rhythmic subdivisions naturally. It's how you play when your body is engaged.

In a group situation, good players have a knack for finding a way to lift the energy of the groove, to keep it alive and fun. This is usually done by putting some emphasis on those up beats and syncopations—whether it's from a rhythm player, such as a drummer or a guitar player, or a melody player, such as a sax player or a singer.

Listen to Stevie Wonder's vocal timing on "I Was Made to Love Her." There is a very strong pulse in this song with nearly equal emphasis on all four beats—what we call "four on the floor." To counteract all that down beat energy, almost every articulation in the vocal is syncopated, accenting the up beats. Focus on the bass part in the Motown classic "Ain't No Mountain High Enough." Listen to the way he brings out the off beats, especially in the verses. The bass part in Marvin Gaye's classic "What's Going On" is an amazing example of the balance between the down beat and up beat energy. The bass lands on the downbeat in every bar of the tune, but the second half of each bar is different, creating a forward motion by emphasizing up beat syncopations. This song also wonderfully demonstrates how to make small variations in a repetitive pattern, the key to good rhythm playing. Both of these bass parts were played by the legendary James Jamerson.

Yes, there is beauty in repetition, but not necessarily in exact repetition.

Variety

Good rhythm players have an instinct for variety. They understand that the human brain is designed to start ignoring things after a short time if they remain static. In addition to the possible shortening of attention spans brought on by our screen-based culture, we also have an ancient survival instinct that filters out non-threatening stimuli to allow us to be better on the alert for danger. If a sound doesn't change, we tune it out. In fact, we often use unchanging background sounds to help fall asleep. That should tell you something about playing rhythm. Don't lull your listeners to sleep, especially if your goal is to get them to dance. It takes something unusual or unexpected to recapture our attention. By attention, I don't mean the rhythm guitar player taking the spotlight from the singer; I mean that to be effective, a groove needs to be listened to. If you tune a groove out, it won't make you move.

What this means for the rhythm player is that the groove needs to change in order to be heard. Yes, there is beauty in repetition, but not necessarily in exact repetition. If a groove doesn't breathe, it stagnates and loses its power.

For string players, many of whom are brand new to rhythm playing, you can think about rhythmic variety as a series of short musical excursions: start with a clear home base groove, allow yourself to wander off by changing the ghosting/accenting, and then return to your home base.

Perfect Imperfections

Luckily, keeping it fresh is more fun than trying to repeat something perfectly. Little things, like playing with the amount of ghosting, can be all it takes to make a groove more infectious. Instead of focusing on consistent perfect execution, a good rhythm player keeps a groove flexible and welcomes all the textural irregularity that comes with handmade music. There is a great deal of humanity that gets expressed through intentional and unintentional inconsistencies.

A good rhythm player keeps a groove flexible and welcomes all the textural irregularity that comes with handmade music.

The inconsistencies I'm talking about here are differences in dynamics—how things are emphasized—and not inconsistencies in timing or tempo. Keeping steady time is sacrosanct in a groove, and any significant inconsistency in the evenness of the rhythm will disrupt the flow and weaken the groove. (See Ch. 5: "Placekeeper Notes—Locking to the Grid.")

Unpredictability

The unpredictability of those irregularities makes a groove interesting and keeps us from tuning it out. Many rhythm players will keep you involved by intentionally throwing in seemingly random accents.

The ultimate example of this principle of unpredictability is be-bop jazz drumming and "comp" piano playing. You're always wondering where the next accent is going to be. It's playful and keeps you delighted in a subtle rhythmic way. And, unsurprisingly, it usually brings out the up beats. It's good energy. Listen to Elvin Jones playing drums and McCoy Tyner on piano with Coltrane in "Bessie's Blues," and try to guess where the accents are going to be. Charlie Parker's recording of "Now's the Time" is another of many examples of unpredictability in jazz rhythm sections.

> *Unpredictability makes a groove interesting and keeps us from tuning it out.*

Improvisation

With grooves, it's not necessary to come up with great new musical ideas all the time. Sometimes all you have to do is respond to someone else, to be reactive. By focusing on the underlying subdivision, the strum, you can shape your groove without losing it. In fact, it's much easier to do that than to keep playing the same thing over and over again as exactly as possible. That's work. You don't work a cello.

Rhythmic improvisation is an easy entry point for more traditional melodic improvisation. Solos don't need to be filled with tons of different notes to be wonderful. You can say a lot with just a few notes. Most drum solos use only a few different pitches but lots of interesting rhythm. This can have enormous emotional and musical impact.

> *Sometimes all you have to do is respond to someone else, to be reactive.*

If you're looking for more ways to start improvising, to get out of your shell, you might start with being playful. Engage in a rhythmic dialogue with other instruments—imitate them or answer them—even if they are only in your imagination.

Play
Superstition

Listen carefully to Stevie Wonder's "Superstition." The main keyboard part is a 2 bar rhythmic riff. It gets repeated many times throughout the song, but it's rarely played exactly the same way twice. There is also a second keyboard part going on at the same time in the left speaker that is constantly changing. This song is a wonderful example of how a simple riff can have hundreds of variations to keep it fresh and more responsive to each moment of the song. Play along with the recording and make up your own variations.

The Yin/Yang of Rhythm

As simple as it sounds—and admittedly this is a broad generalization—up beats bring the energy up, and down beats give it weight. Any good groove is a wonderful balance of down beat weight and an opposing up beat lift.

Bringing out the up beats of the subdivision energizes the groove because it calls attention to its smallest particle, the Groovon. The simple act of taking four beats and turning them into sixteen smaller beats increases the energy level.

Bringing weight to the down beats, however, is just as important. In fact, the weight of the down beat is determined largely by the strength of the opposing up beat energy. The back beat on the two and four is a counterweight to the down beats on one and three. The more strength that goes into the back beat, the heavier the down beat becomes. An especially strong down beat might be preceded by a drum fill or some series of syncopations that increase the down beat's impact by ramping up the strength of the up beats.

In bebop jazz, the bass plays on the strong beats, the quarter note pulse, while the drums, piano and, often, melody instruments accent the syncopated up beats. In pop, the kick drum is usually the weight, and often a syncopated vocal or instrumental melody is the counterweight.

It's the yin/yang of rhythm.

Any good groove is a wonderful balance of down beat weight and an opposing up beat lift.

Brütal Bow Technique 101

A SHORT WORD on metal/extreme music style "riffing" or "chugging"

Like Tracy, I was conservatory trained and I studied with the same descendant line of teachers he did. I studied with Daniel Phillips, Margaret Pardee, and Masao Kawasaki, all of them Galamian acolytes. But I was spending some nights sneaking out and going to underground hardcore shows. My favorite bands growing up were metal and punk bands like Slayer, Anthrax, Metallica, Biohazard, Bad Brains, Cro-Mags, and Minor Threat. However, it wasn't until I was an adult that it occurred to me to try and play metal and punk on my chosen instrument, the violin. As a pioneer in this hybrid, I made many mistakes and missteps that this little introduction will help you to avoid if you're considering this path.

One aspect that must be considered, to piggyback on Tracy's (I mean, Artov D. Grøøve's) discovery of the Groovon, is the exact nature of the particular Groovon specific to the genre one is playing. In extreme music playing, the Groovon is particularly aggressive and on the "front end" of the beat. ALL of the notes in the Groovon are accented. There are no ghost notes. Or rather, it's gotta SEEM that there are no ghost notes. There are secret places that can be unaccented, and secret places to rest, as long as one gives the appearance that when notes are being played, they're being done with complete and unrelenting aggression.

When I was younger, I would tire myself out pretty quickly playing as hard and as fast as I could. It wasn't until many shows and mistakes later that I realized that even if the outer layer of the music requires that I stage-dive or knock down an amplifier, the inner layer of the music still requires me to be calm. A good analogy is the martial arts. One must remain calm and, as the Muay Thai fighters say, "jai yen" and "sabai sabai", or have a cool heart and be relaxed. A good fighter's fists, elbows, kicks, and knees are anything but calm—but their mind is.

All of the rules, guidelines, and suggestions that Tracy outlines in this book remain relevant and are in effect for this particular genre, but perhaps the overall aggression is turned up several notches consistently. Here is a great example to try this idea out:

This exercise is based on a core idea in most modern metal music, showing up in riffs from bands as diverse as Lamb of God to The Dillinger Escape Plan. This should be done slowly at first, making sure the wrist is tight, which runs contrary to standard violin technique. Care should be given to make sure your core muscles are activated, so your hand itself is rather tense, but your shoulders and arms in general are loose and relaxed. Remember to let gravity be your friend.

Imagine if you had a rock tied to a piece of string and you were using that as a weapon. The rock represents your fist, and the piece of string tied to it represents your arm—the string is relaxed and loose, but the hand pummels at will. As soon as you feel fatigue, you should stop. Build your endurance slowly, as this exercise should not be played for long periods of time until one is ready for that. This exercise is potentially hazardous to your health, as improper execution can lead to injury. Good luck!

Earl Maneein
Violin, (SEVEN)SUNS, Black Heart Sutra)
www.earlmaneeinmusic.com

12. Triplets and other Odd-ities
Alternating Accents

See: Groove Study 13

The grid we learned about in Chapter 2 ("The Grid—The Structure of Grooves") is a binary, up/down framework that lends itself well to music in 4/4 or 2/4. But not all music is in 4/4. Luckily, the consistent up/down strum that we've been using in the previous Practice Grooves also applies to triplets, quintuplets and other odd numbered groupings or meters.

Some styles, such as Celtic tunes in 6/8 or 9/8 time and 12/8 blues shuffles, subdivide each beat into groups of three. As with any other application of Strum Bowing, the bow maintains consistent down/up subdivisions. But in odd number groupings, the downbeat accents alternate between down and up bows. For instance:

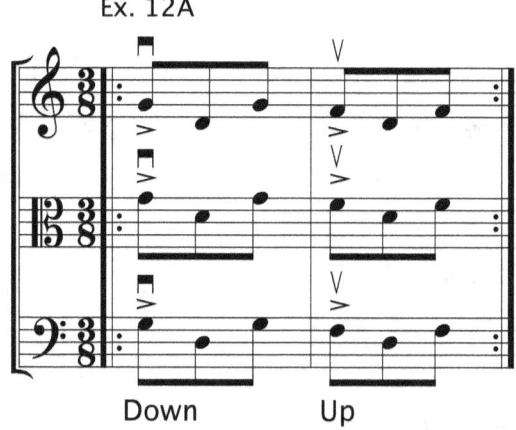

Ex. 12A

Down   Up

As you practice this, try to make the up bow accents equal to the down bow accents. Use your voice to help you.

Spend some time physicalizing this groove. Shift your weight back and forth between your feet on the down beats. Coordinate the down bow accent with the right foot and the up bow accent with the left foot (or vice versa). It may feel a little, well, "odd" at first, but the best way to internalize a groove is to move or dance to it. It helps to have something to dance to, so you could try strumming along to Stevie Wonder's "Higher Ground" or Michael Jackson's "The Way You Make Me Feel." These are good examples of 12/8 grooves.

Notice that in Ex. 12A, the Groovon is the eighth note this time (not the sixteenth note as in the previous examples).

This same rule of maintaining the down/up strum applies to other odd meters, such as fives or sevens. Strum consistent Groovons so that the strong downbeat of each group alternates between down and up bow accents. As you play Ex. 12B, shift your weight back and forth on the downbeats along with the alternating bow accents. As always, use your voice to help you.

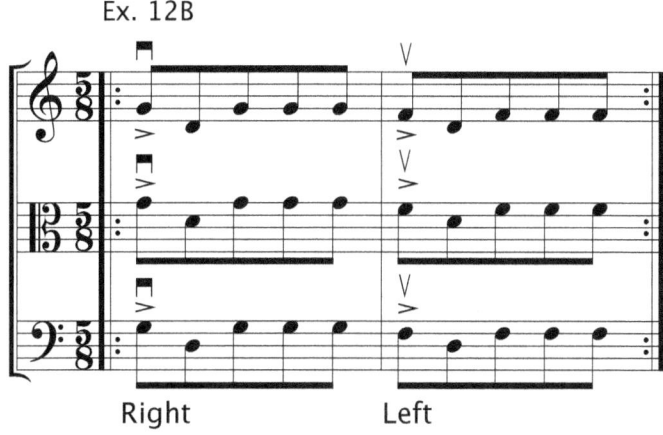

The best way to internalize a groove is to move or dance to it.

It often feels more natural to add a secondary accent in the compound meters of five and seven or more. This is because all odd meters are groups of threes and twos.

Try doing the same exercise, but this time with the secondary accents. Again, use your voice to help direct your arms and feet.

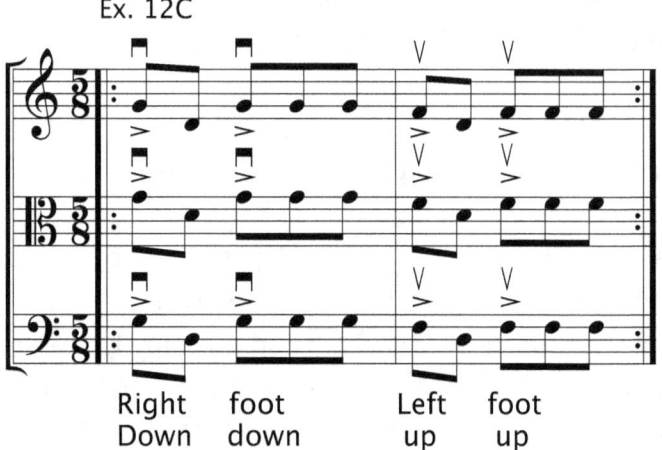

Here it is in seven:

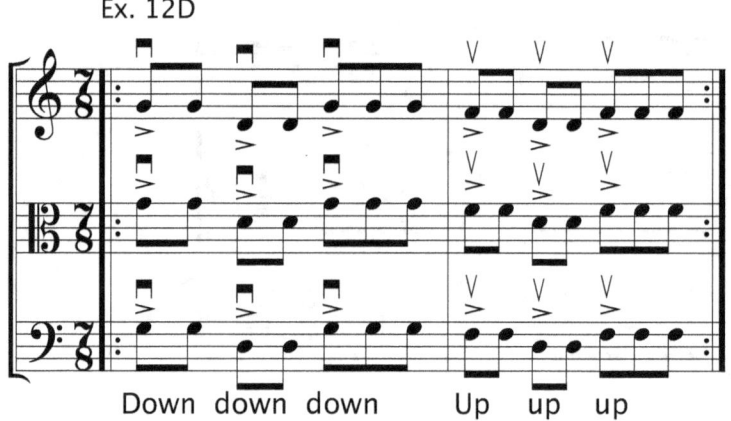

If you subdivide the Groovon from eighth notes to sixteenth notes, the bowing reverts back to down bows on down beats. Instead of three notes, like this:

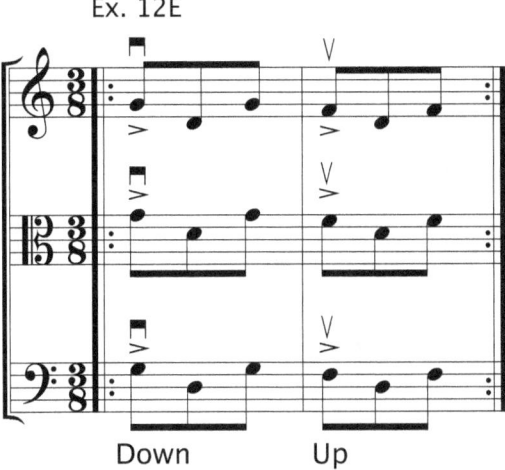

...there are six.

Instead of five notes like this:

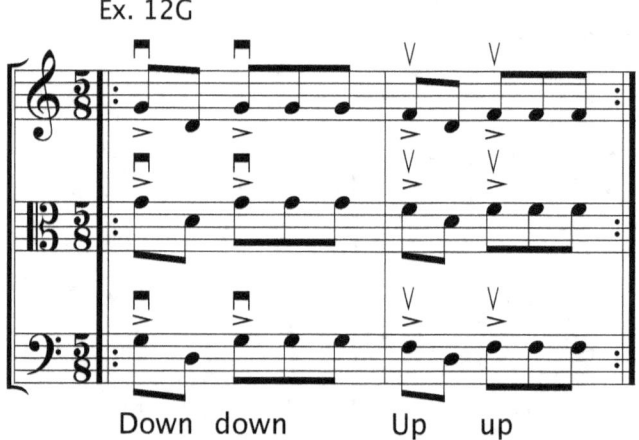

...there are ten.

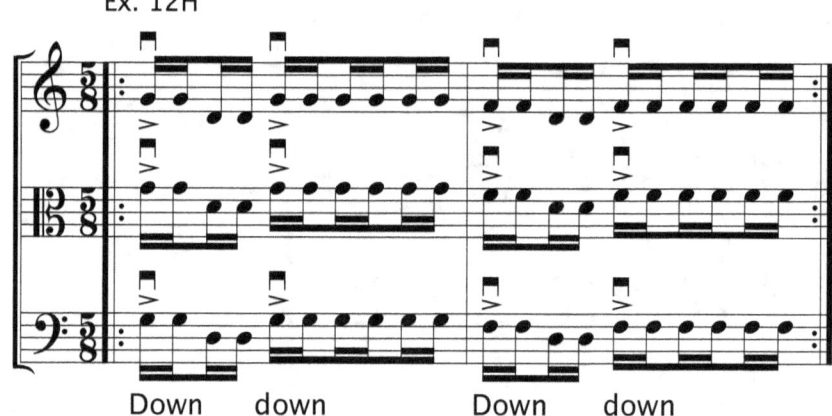

And instead of seven notes like this:

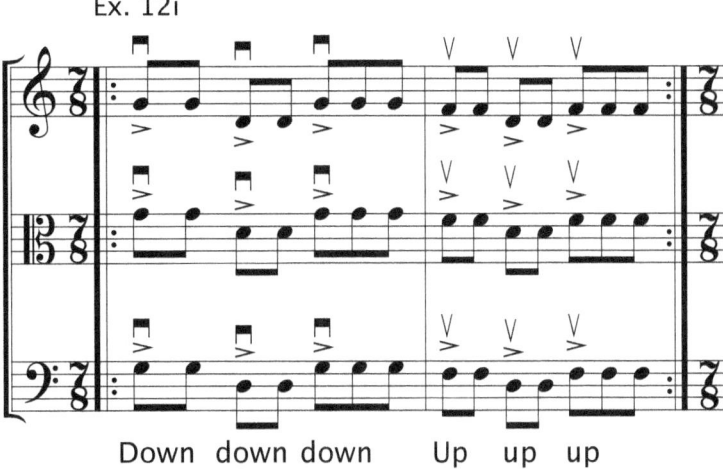

...there are fourteen.

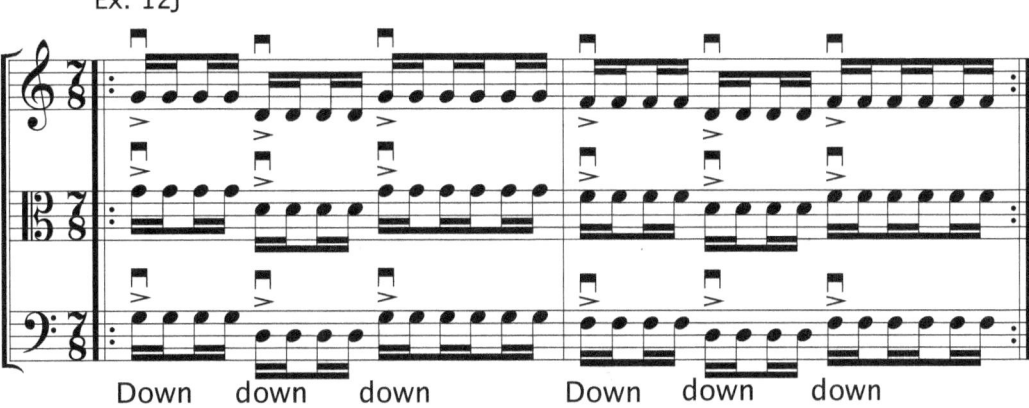

Here's where odd meters get really interesting. When you double-time them, they turn into cross rhythms. This rhythm:

Ex. 12K

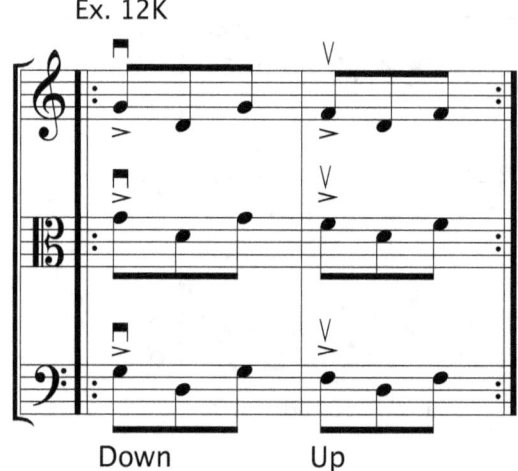

Down   Up

...turns into this:

Ex. 12L

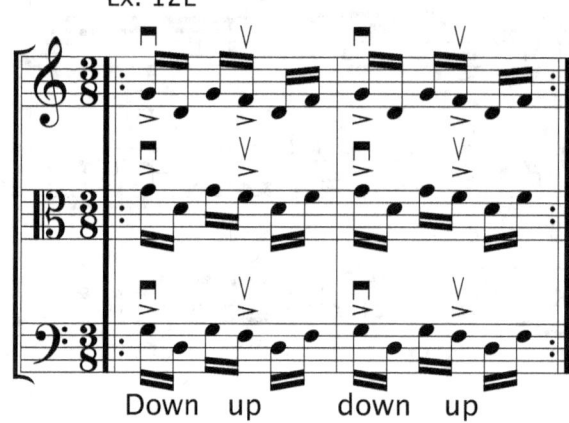

Down   up   down   up

When you play Ex. 12L, be sure to accent the alternating down and up bows. Use your voice to help you. But instead of only physicalizing the accents, this time physicalize the eighth note beat with your feet and the accents with your arms. You can tap your foot or bounce a little or step back and forth. This will help you internalize and physicalize the eighth note pulse. It may take a minute or two to coordinate, but the accents you play will create a cross rhythm to the steady 3/8 pulse. It's simple math: 6

can divide into two groups of three, or three groups of two.

This rhythm is commonly known as *three against two*, and it's used in a lot of African music. What makes it so fundamental is that it achieves a simple balance between the downbeat and the syncopated up beat accent.

Let's apply this same concept to our 5/8 and 7/8 examples. This bar of 5/8:

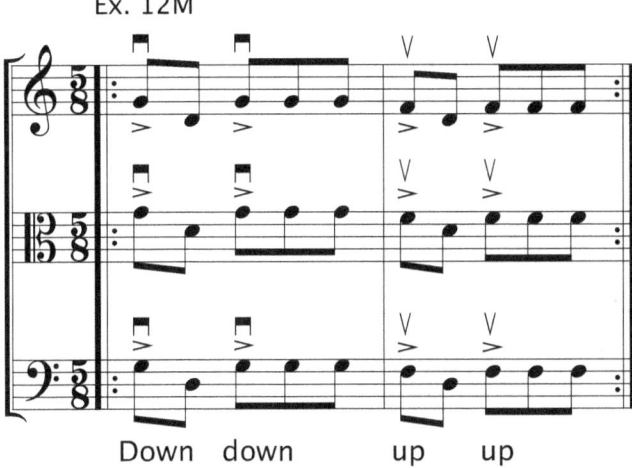

...becomes this:

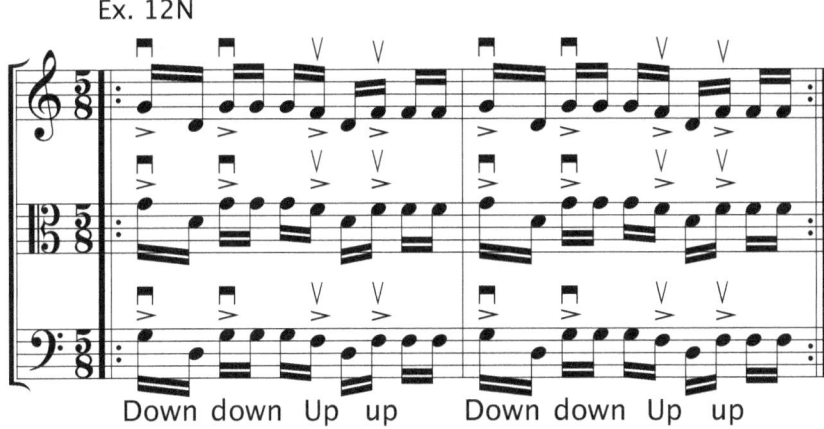

Triplets and other Odd-ities

And this bar of 7/8:

Ex. 12o

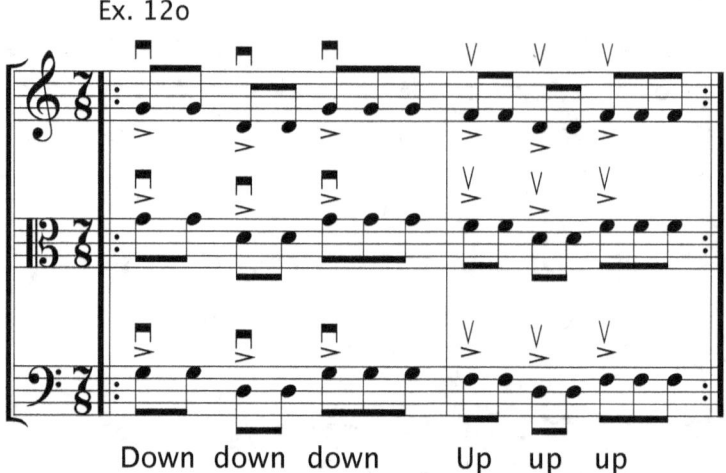

Down down down Up up up

...becomes this:

Ex. 12P

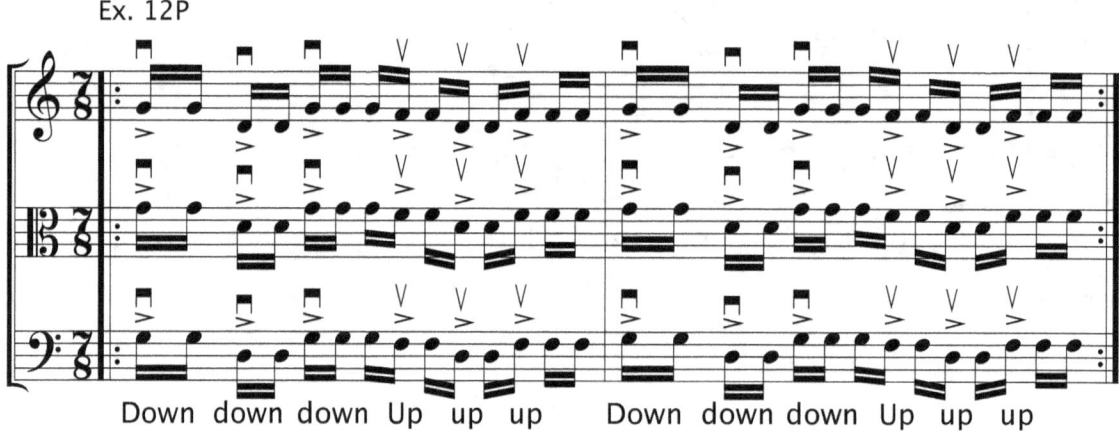

Down down down Up up up   Down down down Up up up

One of the results of these cross rhythms is that the second half of the bar is highly syncopated because the accents reverse and fall on the up beats.

102   Triplets and other Odd-ities

Threes and Twos

The key to odd meters is that they all break down to groups of threes and twos. For instance, a famous use of 5/8 is the theme from Mission Impossible.

EX. 12Q

But while the pulse is in eighth notes, there is a cross rhythm that happens when the subdivisions are grouped into threes and twos. It's actually the same as the 3/8 cross rhythm in Ex 12L but with 2 extra beats added.

Ex. 12R

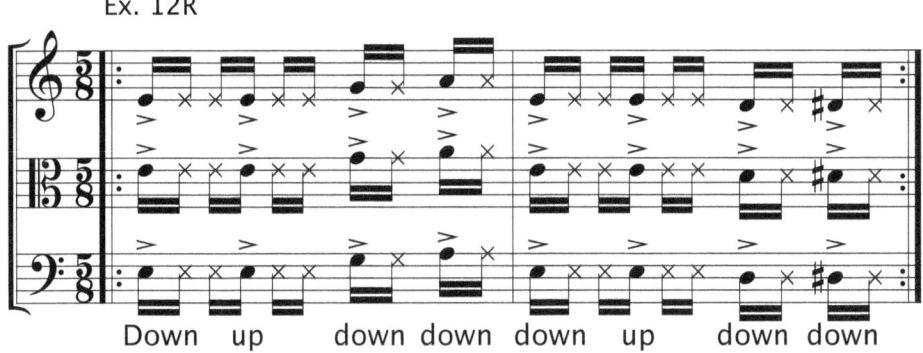

Triplets and other Odd-ities

Exceptions to Every Rule

Most grooves work better if the bow direction comes from Strum Bowing with each subdivision played by separate bows. There are times, however, when another bowing just feels better. Here is an example of an exception to the rule:

In 12/8 each beat is divided into 3 subdivisions. Let's say you want to play these up beat accents from Stevie Wonder's "Higher Ground" like this:

Ex. 12S

Use your GPS, find the Groovon, ghost all the placekeeper notes and bring out the accents like this:

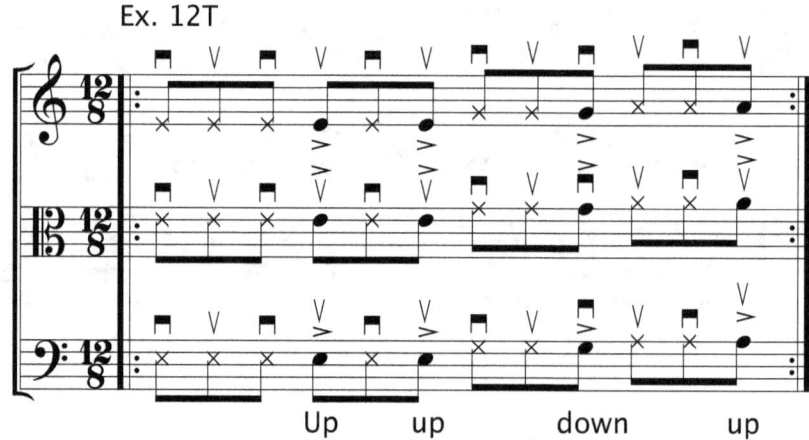
Ex. 12T

This leaves you with this bow direction key:

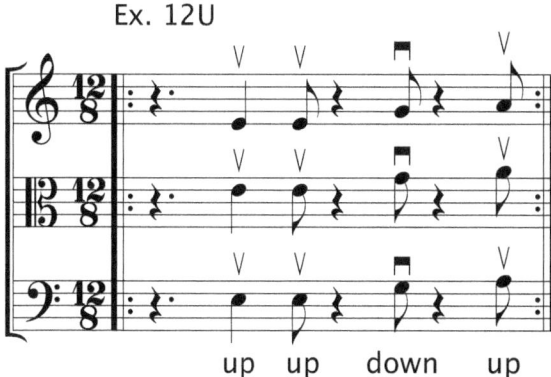

But even after repeatedly shouting bow direction commands to my arm, this bowing never felt comfortable to me. It just feels more natural to play it like this:

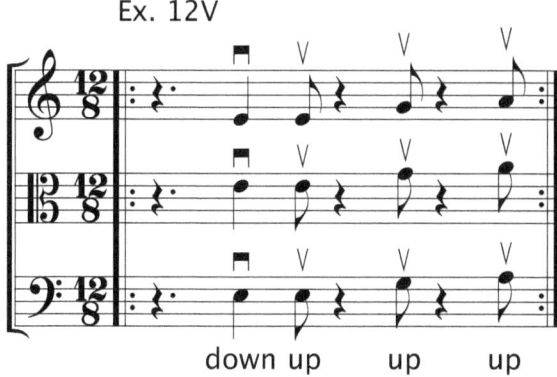

But there's actually a reason it feels more natural with this bowing, and it's pretty common for triplet patterns. It's because your body feels the triplets as swung eighths in 4/4.

...which adheres to a down/up grid and is a clear example of, you guessed it, Strum Bowing. No wonder it feels so natural.

Part II:
The Vertical Strum
The Chop and Beyond

13. Going Vertical—Part 1
The Chop

See: Groove Study 14

More percussion— more better.

The Chop is the vertical form of Strum Bowing. It is a non-pitched percussive sound. We can isolate it and use it as a simple back beat, or we can adapt it into a non-pitched version of Strum Bowing, complete with accents and ghosts. Once we develop the Chop, we can combine it with the horizontal Strum Bowing we learned in the first half of this book to create something I call a *3D Strum*.

The advantages of the non-pitched Chop are 1) like any non-pitched percussion instrument, you can easily play in any key and over the most difficult chord changes; and 2) more percussion—more better.

The History of the Chop

The Chop originated with bluegrass fiddlers. String bands typically had no drums or percussion, so the mandolin or guitar player would often mute their strings and make a percussive back beat on their instrument. Fiddlers picked up on the idea and started making bow slaps in the middle of the bow. Iconic fiddler Richard Greene, who played with the father of bluegrass, Bill Monroe, modified the technique by migrating it to the frog where he could then integrate it into other pitched and non-pitched rhythms. Greene later taught this technique to Darol Anger, who developed his own Chop vocabulary and has become one of the masters of the craft. Another amazing chopper is Casey Driessen, who has taken it to yet another level, including Triple Chops, forward and backward Scrapes and detailed notation about bow placement. Rushad Eggleston has done similar ground breaking work developing the chop on the cello.

The Out Bow

I refer to all chop-related bow strokes as vertical, as opposed to the traditional horizontal bow strokes we've used so far in this book. String players are not conventionally taught to use the bow vertically. There is a vertical element to spiccato and other off-the-string strokes, but even with these bow strokes, the sound is always produced horizontally. With the Chop, the sound is produced in a very different way. It's not a down bow. It's an out bow.

OK, finally! The moment you've been waiting for...

> **Chop**
>
> Also referred to here as the Simple Chop. A non-pitched vertical bow stroke consisting of a down stroke and an audible up stroke.

The Down Stroke

For the basic down stroke, you are going to throw the bow onto the string and leave it there. To guide you, here are the Five Rules of The Chop, which I've adapted from what Darol Anger taught me when I first joined the Turtle Island String Quartet.

Five Rules of The Chop

1. **At the frog** The placement of the stroke is at the very bottom of the bow, as low in the bow as you can get without hitting the metal ferrule at the frog.
2. **Hair out** Rotate the bow so the hair is away from you. This rotation causes the bow to skid away from you a tiny bit when it hits the string. That tiny skid is what produces the chop sound. On violin and viola, that means the stick is toward you and the hair is toward the fingerboard. On cello and bass, the stick is toward you and the hair is toward the bridge.
3. **Right hand loose** Keep your bow grip relaxed and loose so that the bow is free to skid as it hits the strings. Otherwise it won't make much, if any, sound.
4. **Dampen the strings** Dampen the strings with the left hand. (See Ch. 4: "Ghost Notes—How to *Not* Play An Instrument.") Don't push the strings down all the way or you will hear pitched notes.
5. **Leave bow on the strings** After you throw the bow onto the strings, leave it right there. Don't bounce it. This is so you can then make a sound with the up stroke.

As you try out this new stroke, review the five rules above to keep yourself on track.

🎥 Ex 13A

What you are shooting for is a completely non-pitched "chuck" that sounds a little bit like a snare drum. Practice for consistency of tone and dynamics. You can Chop on any string you like, and it's often a good idea to land on 2 strings at once so you can throw the bow a little harder. Eventually, you can vary which strings you use to change the sound slightly and create a more nuanced groove.

If you keep a death grip on your bow, it can't skid. To compensate, you may try to push the bow onto the string. This is about as effective as pushing a drum stick onto a drum head.

Troubleshooting Tips:

- The most common issue is with rule number three, keeping the right hand loose. To get a sound, it's necessary to hold the bow loosely so that you can release your bow grip just as the bow meets the string. This allows it to skid. If you keep a death grip on your bow, it can't skid. To compensate, you may try to push the bow onto the string. This is about as effective as pushing a drum stick onto a drum head. Or, you may try to get a chop-like sound with an aggressive marcato stroke. That may be a really cool sound, but it's not a chop. You have to throw the bow instead, as if you want it to bounce, like a ricochet stroke—except it doesn't bounce; it skids because it's not a down bow, it's an out bow.

- You probably have to throw the bow down harder than you think. Hold onto your violin securely so you don't worry about dropping it. Then, lift your bow, and use your wrist to throw the bow down hard. A chop doesn't always have to be loud, of course, but in order to learn how to do it, you should try to get as loud and solid a sound as possible. You won't hurt your bow or your violin.

- Is your bow hair still turned away from you? Many string players rotate their bow the opposite way for conventional playing, with the stick of the bow away from them, in order to play with the edge of the bow hair. Muscle memory may take over, so you may have to keep reminding yourself to rotate your bow so that the stick faces in and the hair faces out.

The Up Stroke

The reason we leave the bow on the string after the chop (rule number five) is so that we can then make a sound when we pick it back up. Pull the bow up off the string with a quick jerking motion with your fingers and wrist so that it catches the string and makes a non-pitched, short percussive noise similar to the noise of the down stroke. It's almost like pizzicato with the bow. Practice this until you can make the up stroke as loud as the down stroke.

🎥 Ex. 13B

Pain is No Gain

If it hurts, stop! Watch out for straining your right arm. Some people may feel tension in their forearm or elbow, and others may feel it in their wrist or hand. This is because these muscles are being used in a new and repetitive way, creating a perfect environment for carpal tunnel syndrome or other tendonitis-related problems to creep in. Be careful—if it starts to hurt, stop immediately and wait a day or two before you try it again. Practice in short sessions. In time, as you develop the stroke, you'll be able to get a better Chop sound with less effort and tension.

It's almost like pizzicato with the bow.

The Simple Chop

I call this combination of down and up stroke a *Simple Chop*. The Simple Chop is very useful, and when we double-time it, it becomes what I call a *Compound Chop* (See Ch. 14: "Going Vertical Part 2—The Compound Chop"), a vertical strum that we can integrate into the rest of our Strum Bowing.

The Chop: Relaxing the Right Hand

I'M NOT SURE about the difference between discovery and invention. In my case, the Chop started out as an accidental discovery, then I kept doing it, not really understanding it.

My first gig as a professional bluegrass player was with the Greenbriar Boys circa 1964-65 and Bob Yellin, our banjo player, asked me to do that "driving rhythm thing". Then I joined Bill Monroe in 1966 with the clear intention to be the disciple at the feet of the Grand Master. He was fine with this. Throughout my approximately one year tenure as a Bluegrass Boy we had developed a great and jovial relationship. We threw each other a lot of wisecracks, but whenever he suggested anything musical, either verbally or through his mandolin, I utterly and without ego absorbed like a sponge, no questions or doubts. He was the Guru. That was why I was there—to learn Bluegrass from the Inventor. So one day, he says "Ritchid, just play rhythm and solos for a few months. No fills." No problem. I was thirsty and grateful for any music related utterance. I really rushed a lot and this was his cure.

Now I need to describe my different approaches to bluegrass rhythm fiddle, most of them backbeat related. First, there is the simple tap or slap on every backbeat with the tip of the bow. Sometimes if you release the bow grip a little you get a ricochet sort of fluttering which can be controlled by slightly tightening your grip at certain strategic moments. This could either contain pitch or not, depending on whether or not you muffle the strings with the left hand.

Second, there is the brush stroke near the middle of the bow. This was masterfully executed by Mack Magaha, a member of Porter Wagoner's band, and he also played with Reno and Smiley. Mack could be considered one of Chop's distant ancestors, not quite chopping but using double and triple stops to play rhythm. Here in addition to a brush you could also do a sort of bouncing spiccato.

Third, is a backbeat short chunk played at the frog, all down bows.

And fourth is The Chop. The Chop was born out of necessity as well as invention. Bill's sets could run as long as 75 minutes, sometimes even more if there were lots of encores. Occasionally, in a club we could play up to six 45-minute sets a night. It was there that I realized that the Chop was really a lazy thing and could be performed with any level of fatigue. The tip slap, middle of the bow semi-spiccato and the hard down bow hit on every backbeat all require a lot of control involving the extended use of wrist muscles. Then there would be lots of pain if that's all you did for an hour except when you played a short solo somewhere in a song. But if you do a slightly lazy down bow chunk at the frog with very little wrist control and then lift the bow to do it again—Voila! A free sound occurs: the Pinch! This I could do all night—just drop the bow near the frog and lift it up. Two sounds: the Chop and the Pinch. Remember that the Pinch happens because of a lazy lift up. Once this was understood, one could then analyze and perfect each movement, and then, most importantly, involve the left hand in the process.

This is how I developed the use of the chop to play melodies in addition to its simple rhythm-keeping function. Explaining how the left hand functions is another matter. Here, I'm only telling the story of the right hand.

Richard Greene
Violinist, legendary "Inventor of the Chop"
www.richardgreene.net

14. Going Vertical—Part 2
The Compound Chop

See: Groove Study 15, Groove Study 16

> **Compound Chop**
>
> A double-time version of the Simple Chop in which the first note is stressed and the other 3 are not.

In order to integrate the Chop into Strum Bowing, we need to be able to play Groovons using the vertical stroke. The Compound Chop allows us to strum vertically just as we learned to strum horizontally in the first half of this book.

Once we get comfortable with this new vertical strum, we can begin to mix it with the horizontal strum for a hybrid of horizontal and vertical strokes that I call 3-D Strumming.

Compound Interest

First, let's review the Simple Chop we just learned in Chapter 13. It consists of a short, percussive sound on both the down stroke and the up stroke.

Ex. 14A

In learning the Simple Chop, I encouraged you to lift your bow and throw it down hard. This was to make sure the mechanics of the stroke were in place to get the correct feeling and sound of the Chop. But, I also mentioned that the Chop doesn't have to be loud. As you play Ex. 14A above, start to play more quietly. Don't throw the bow as hard, don't lift it as far from the strings and economize your motions and bow usage. Gradually, let the tempo get faster, like a truck on a slight downhill. Don't force it; just let it creep faster and faster as the motions become smaller and it gets more comfortable. Give yourself some time with this. Work in short sessions. You may have to stop, rest your arm and come back to it a few times.

Let's fast forward a few weeks in your life to when you have doubled your tempo. Let's think of the rhythm as sixteenths rather than eighths.

🎥 Ex. 14B

As you play this sixteenth note chop, add an accent on the first of each group of four Groovons.

🎥 Ex. 14C

> **Power Stroke**
>
> The first, heaviest stroke of the Compound Chop.

Power Stroke, Rest Stroke

Let's call that first accent the Power Stroke. As you work on bringing out the accent on the Power Stroke, you will discover that you have to contend with the down stroke on the third Groovon and try to keep it from being as strong as the first Groovon. You may find yourself avoiding it by barely placing your bow on the strings. Let's call this third Groovon the Rest Stroke. In between the Power Stroke and the Rest Stroke are two unaccented placekeeper up strokes that keep us accurately lined up on the grid.

If we zoom in on the microscopic level of one beat, it would look like this:

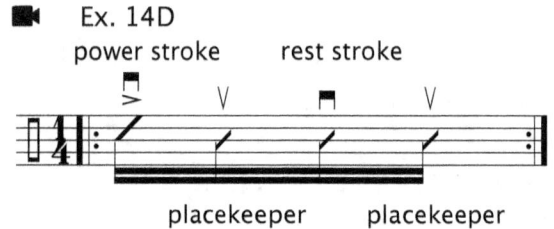

Ex. 14D

> **Rest Stroke**
>
> The third, unstressed stroke of the Compound Chop.

Troubleshooting Tips:

- As we learned with the Simple Chop, we rotate the hair away from us so that the bow will skid and make a sound. If we want to reduce the sound, all we have to do is rotate the hair back toward us to a flat position and it won't skid. Exaggerate this motion by throwing the bow down and out a little closer to the fingerboard for the Power Stroke and then rotating the hair flat, quietly placing the Rest Stroke a bit closer to the bridge. The inertia of this back and forth motion will keep your vertical strum steady. Cellos and basses are the reverse: Power Stroke closer to the bridge and Rest Stroke closer to the fingerboard.

- Gradually let this pattern speed up. Soon, it will start to become muscle memory. Work towards the evenness of accents and ghosts.

The Back Beat

Let's fast forward a few more weeks in your life. Once you have the Compound Chop under control, you can take it up a notch by adding a back beat. All that means is that you put a heavier accent on the second and fourth beats. If you listen to some dance-based grooves, most of them will have a strong back beat, usually played by a snare drum or some electronic equivalent of it.

▶Ex. 14E

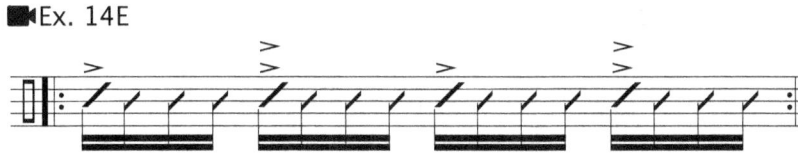

Back Beat

The second and fourth beats in a 4/4 meter.

Play
Imitate Percussion

Your bow is a highly refined tool capable of producing limitless subtleties of articulation and dynamics. Explore the variety of accents and ghosts that are possible with vertical strokes. Experiment with different amounts of bow pressure and different fingers for left hand dampening. Try Chopping on different strings. See if you can make different percussion sounds—a low sound for a kick drum, a loud Chop for the snare, ghosted up strokes for the hi-hat. Listen to the drums or percussion on random songs, and try to imitate the variety of different instruments and drum sounds. As always, use your voice to help you by beatboxing the groove you are trying to imitate. Take your playing from 2 or 3 shades of accents to hundreds of different shades. Go hi-res.

Chopping on Cello vs. Violin

TRACY TOLD ME he noticed it often takes cellists longer to get the chop to sound good in workshops, and that he theorized that it must be harder on the cello than it is on violin. Tracy is correct (about pretty much everything), but particularly about the fact that the violin is a simpler instrument to play, intended for simpler people. :) In contrast, the sophistication of the cello requires training, mastery, and maturity. For the elite musicians reading this book (a.k.a. cellists), there are a few concepts and technical differences that are helpful to explore:

- Cello often requires more bow arm weight to activate the sound than violin does. For slow/medium tempo grooves, the chop will sound stronger and cleaner using primarily arm weight, originating from the upper arm, rather than slapping at the string from just the hand/wrist. For faster grooves using quicker motions, I hold my arm weight in the air more and balance the bow sensitively in the hand (without grabbing) in order to use mostly finger muscles to guide the bow as my arm motions hinge from the elbow.

- On cello, we can create a metallic slap of the string against the fingerboard by chopping hard with the bow. This can be very loud and satisfying, but often happens randomly if one is not careful. It is worth being intentional about saving the slap/chop combo (what I like to call the "Super Chop") for when you're REALLY rocking out, and maintain a clean "slap-less chop" for most of the time.

- Since chopping is an outward motion (away from the body), that means that by traveling EXTRA far forward, cellists can get a wicked awesome ponticello chop sound! Since we have to move further/faster to accomplish this, it works great when playing a particularly intense groove. The cello provides us a luxurious amount of real estate between the end of the fingerboard and the bridge, and it behooves us to explore all the sonic options available to us as a result of various chopping bow placements!

I could keep going on about all the things that make cello better than violin, but this may not be the time/place … :) I'm just grateful to Tracy for writing this book, and for thinking to include a cello-focused moment in it. My only parting thought is to not underestimate the benefits of a restrained chop pattern that includes some silent spaces. A dense rhythmic pattern that fills every subdivision works when playing by yourself, like when accompanying singing, but it may not leave breathing room for other musicians to join you effectively. Speaking of which, when playing with a drummer or percussionist, I highly recommend NOT CHOPPING! :)

Mike Block (Silk Road Ensemble),
Assoc. Prof., Berklee College of Music
www.mikeblockmusic.com

15. Groovin' the Chop
Vertical Grooves

See: Groove Study 17

Let's go back to the 3 practice grooves from chapters 8, 9 and 10 and see if we can play them with vertical strokes instead of horizontal ones. When we play these grooves with vertical strokes, it doesn't matter what the notes are. We are playing only the rhythm of the groove as if we were playing a non-pitched percussion instrument instead of a violin.

Practice Groove 1

Here is Practice Groove 1 from Chapter 8 ("GPS: Groove Proficiency System—Practice Groove 1"):

Ex. 15A

Here is how we actually play it with the added placekeeper ghost notes:

Ex. 15B

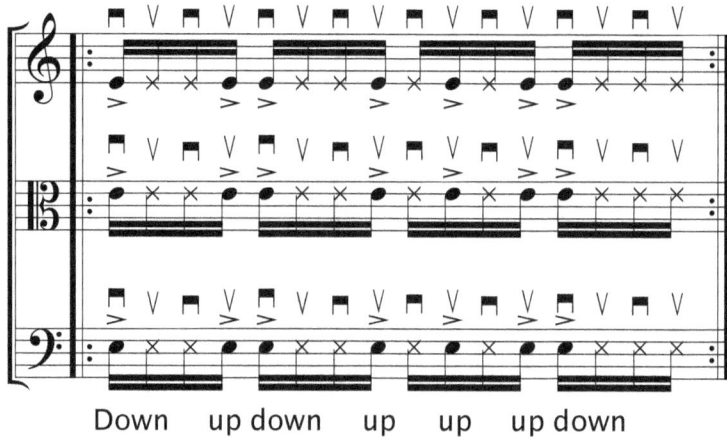

Down　up down　up　up　up down

To play this same groove as a vertical chop, start by playing a Compound Chop.

Ex. 15C

Now, play the accents of Practice Groove 1. Use your voice to help.

Ex. 15D

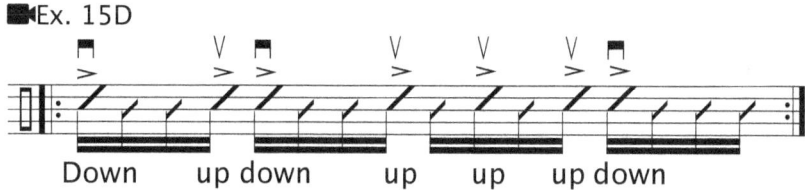

Down　up down　up　up　up down

Practice Groove 2

Let's apply this same process to Practice Groove 2 from Chapter 9 ("GPS: Groove Proficiency System—Practice Groove 2"). Here's the shorthand version:

...which we actually play like this with added placekeeper notes:

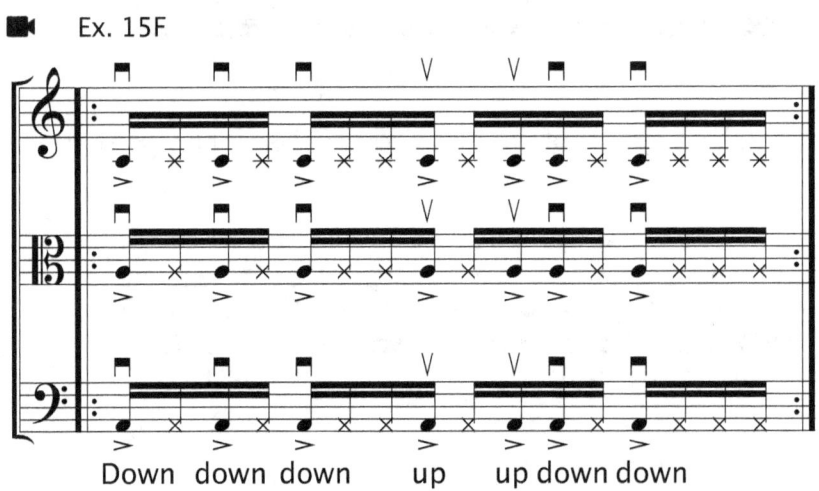

...and which can be played vertically like this:

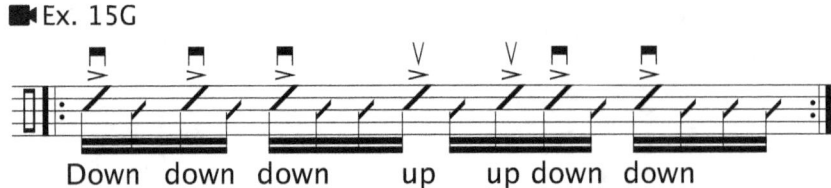

Practice Groove 3

Here's Practice Groove 3 from chapter 10 ("GPS: Groove Proficiency System—Practice Groove 3"):

Ex. 15H

Here it is with the ghosted placekeeper notes:

Ex. 15i

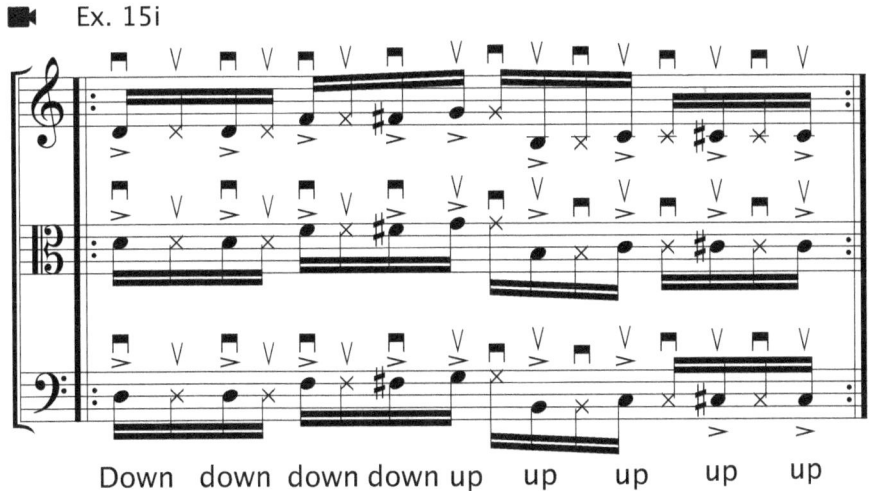

And here it is as a vertical Chop pattern:

Ex. 15J

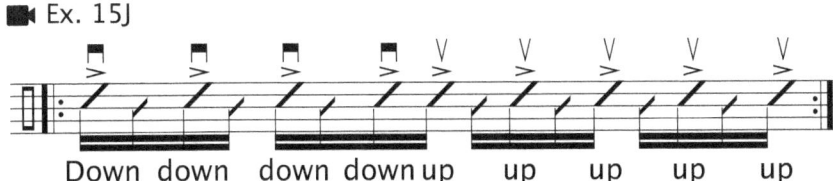

Groovin' the Chop

Play
Variations on a Chop

Play the vertical version of Practice Groove 2 (Ex. 15G) that we just worked on above. As you repeat it over and over, allow the accents to change, and let it mutate to a different groove pattern. You could add a back beat or a new syncopation. Think of it as variations on a theme. This is the same process we used in Chapter 11 ("Variety is the Spice of Grooves—The Power of the Strum.") Try making up new variations with your voice and then imitating them on your instrument. Always strive to make it as rhythmically steady as possible. Practice with a metronome, or play along with a recording. Try making up variations on the vertical Chop version of Practice Groove 3 (Ex. 15 J) as well. Feel free to change things and get creative.

String Drumming

TODAY'S LEADERS in the eclectic styles string field approach the bow hand as an independent leader and partner to the fingering hand rather than an asleep-at-the-wheel but proficient supporter. A driving, rhythmic groove has always been fundamental to roots traditions throughout the world, but the bow patterns per style are generally just as habitual as with classical training.

The imbalance between the two hands is understandable. We are preoccupied with intonation from day one, while bow control focuses on good form and tone followed by mostly symmetrical, style-appropriate bow strokes. Melody and harmony tend to reign supreme, and as a result, we've emerged with a severe shortage of rhythmic skills or, for that matter, right-hand equality to the fingering hand.

When it comes to mastering basic or complex rhythms and rhythmic phrases, it's best to start with an ears-first, bow hand only practice plan. There are a few reasons for this.

The visual cortex, the part of the brain in charge of visual activity, is far larger than the auditory cortex. Science has proven that when the eyes are activated, the other senses can shut down as much as seventy-five percent. To provide one hundred percent of your listening and kinesthetic focus to build new rhythmic skills, refer to a written phrase, play it a few times to lock it in, then turn away from the music stand to repeat the phrase a number of times on an open string before you add left-hand activity.

It's also advantageous to leave the left hand out of your rhythmic warm-ups. Only add it back in when you're confident you've mastered the rhythmic pattern. You are actually building new brain cells in your left motor cortex when you isolate your bow hand. You're also strengthening neural connections between the rhythmic centers of the brain and your right-hand moves and grooves. The control centers for pitch can be found in their own, discrete areas of the brain.

Rhythmizing the Bow

There's so much more to rhythmizing the bow—to quote the title of my DVD—than practicing rhythmic phrases. Any given pattern can sound completely unique each time you modify how you enter and exit each note, where you place inflection (accentuation) within the phrase, whether or not you cut certain notes short—and how you accomplish that, physically

speaking—and the underlying "rhythmic subtext" you feel and hear while playing the phrase.

I used the term, rhythmic subtext, to describe in part what Tracy refers to as Groovons. The rhythmic subtext contains all the ingredients of the style: phrasing, preferred note values and lengths, inflections that tend to repeat for that style, and more. This is why it's so important to listen to artists that personify the style you're interested in to ascertain how the band or ensemble moves and grooves behind the melody. For instance, when playing the fiddle music of Appalachia, if you don't hear and feel a constant shuffle stroke—a long, short, short bow pattern with the inflection on the first of the two short bows—you won't be able to capture the feel of the style. If you don't hear a triplet subtext when playing swing or even Celtic, you won't phrase the music properly. And there are styles too complex to describe here. Thus, the importance of listening carefully.

Here are a few practice techniques to experiment with:
- Move an accent from the first note of a rhythmic phrase to the second, the third, and so on with each repetition.
- Repeat this exercise this time shortening instead of accenting the note.
- Reiterate and each sweep through, substitute a note with a rest.
- Sight-read a different piece of music each day without your left hand. Only play the rhythms.

Julie Lyonn Lieberman
Performer/Author/Educator, Artistic Director: Strings Without Boundaries
www.julielyonn.com

16. The 3-D Strum—Part 1
Horizontal and Vertical Combined

See: Groove Study 18

It may be a little tricky at first to change gears from the vertical out bow to the more traditional down bow.

Let's fast-forward another month or so in your life. You've mastered horizontal and vertical strumming. Now, you're ready to combine the two.

First, play a Simple Chop.

Ex. 16A

Now, add a horizontal stroke on the first beat.

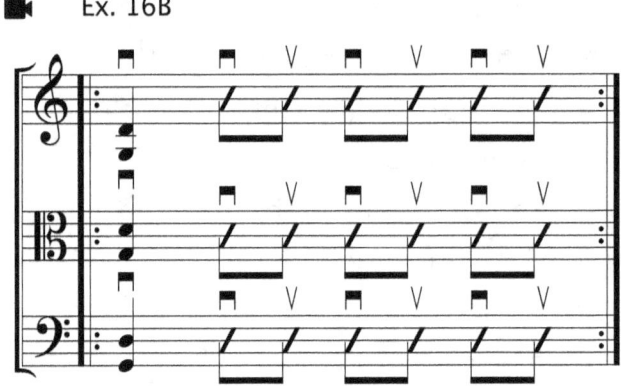
Ex. 16B

Since the Chop takes place exclusively at the frog, you will play the horizontal notes at the frog as well. This will probably be a new feeling for most string players, so you may want to practice playing at the frog without the Chop first to get comfortable with it.

It may be a little tricky at first to change gears from the vertical out bow to the more traditional down bow. Remember to dampen the strings with your left hand for the Chops but to lift the dampening fingers for the horizontal down beat stroke. Try to get a clean contrast between the horizontal pitched notes and the vertical non-pitched Chops.

Double time the Simple Chop to make it a Compound Chop.

Ex. 16C

Add a horizontal note on the downbeat, just as before. You can also start to bring out the back beat on the second and fourth beats.

Ex. 16D

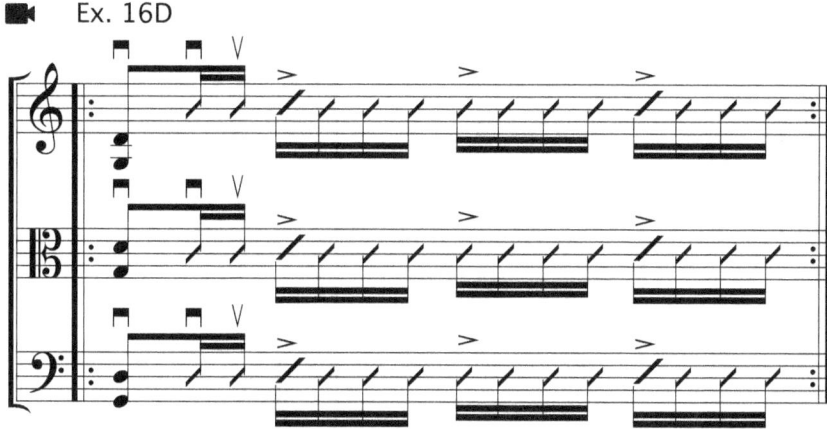

Now, instead of one horizontal eighth note on the down beat, play two eighth notes.

Ex. 16E

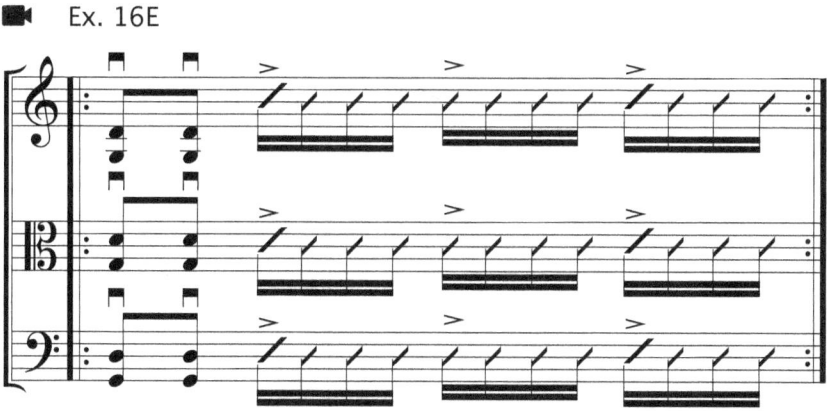

Notice that we are leaving out the placekeeper notes on the first beat. It is virtually impossible to add placekeepers between those 2 horizontal down bows at the frog, so let's just consider those to be implied Groovons.

17. The 3-D Strum—Part 2
3-D Versions of the Practice Grooves

See: Groove Study 19

You've just finished learning the basics of the 3-D Strum, grooves that combines vertical and horizontal bow strokes. Let's practice it with some grooves we are already familiar with.

Practice Groove 1

We'll pick up where we left off in Chapter 15 ("Grooving the Chop—Vertical Grooves"). We took our Practice Groove 1

Ex. 17A

...and learned how to play it vertically like this:

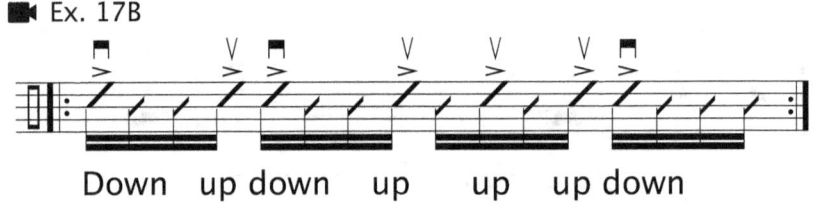

Ex. 17B

Down   up down   up   up   up down

Now let's turn those vertical accents back into horizontal notes. Remember to play it all at the frog.

Ex. 17C

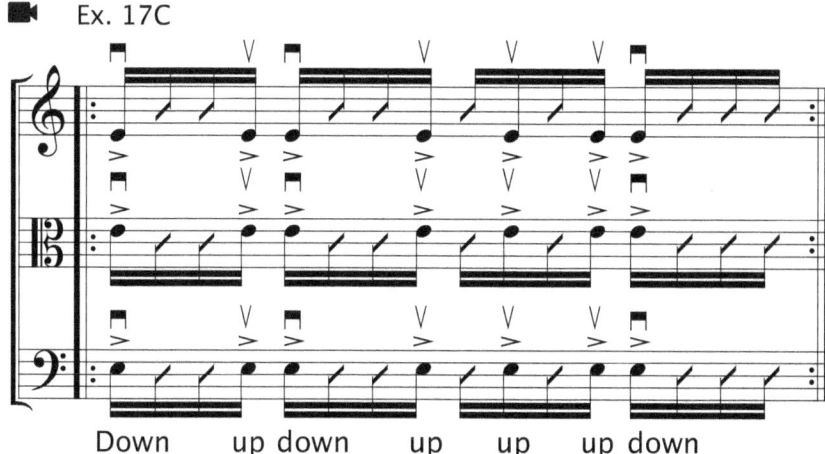

Notice that there is a considerable amount of up beat energy built into this groove with all the syncopation on those up bows.

You can take this groove one step further by putting a heavy Chop back beat on the second and fourth beats to balance all that up beat syncopation. Use your left hand to dampen the strings for the vertical Chops but open the strings up to ring on the horizontal strokes. Slow it down if you need to. Use your voice to help you. If you can say it, you can play it!

Ex. 17D

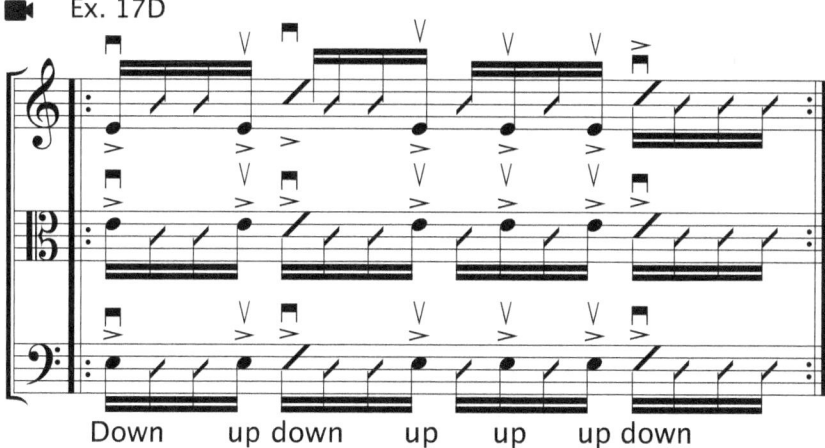

The 3-D Strum—Part 2

Practice Groove 2

Now let's do the same process for Practice Groove 2 from Chapter 9.

Here's the original riff:

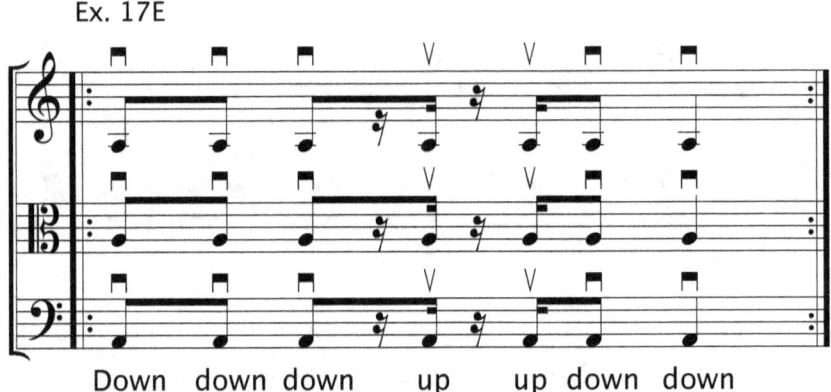

Now play the groove vertically like this:

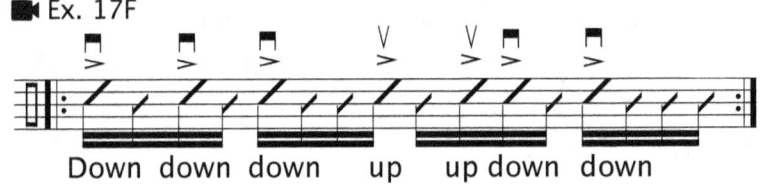

Let's turn those accents into horizontal bass notes. Notice that I've left out a few of the placekeeper notes in the first and third beats. Sometimes you need to leave out a note or two when you're shifting gears from horizontal to vertical. Remember to keep it all at the frog.

Ex. 17G

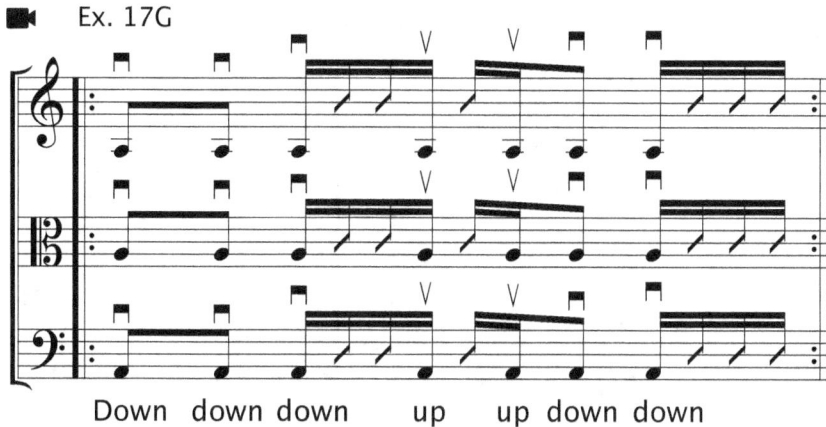

Down down down   up   up down down

Now let's replace the bass notes on the backbeats with heavy Chops.

Ex. 17H

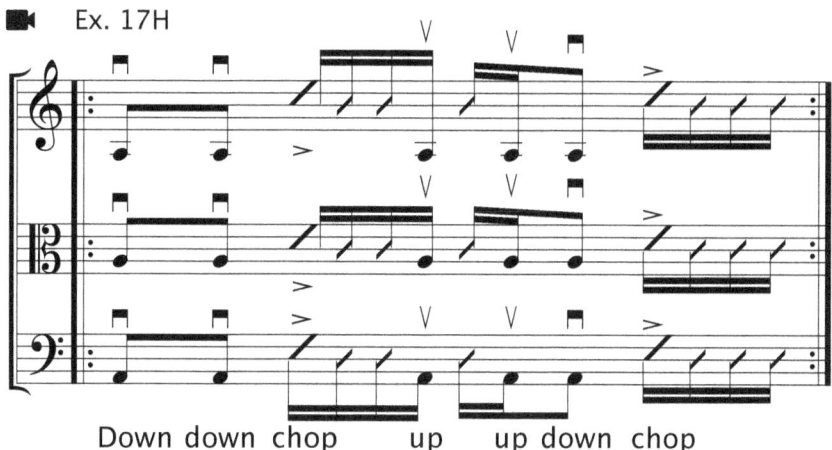

Down down chop   up   up down chop

The Vertical Vector

VERTICAL USE OF THE BOW is becoming an integral part of modern string playing with the advent and development of the ever-expanding realm of "chopping." In this way of playing, the bow moves vertically to and from the string. There is also an important vertical component of the typical horizontal bow stroke that serves to enhance rhythm and tone production. This vertical use of the bow is a bit harder to notice because the bow doesn't actually move up and down – the movement is only in the bow arm.

To train young students to become aware of the bow's vertical component, first I ask them to play continuous sixteenth notes in the middle of their bow. Then, I have them put their bow on the string and pretend to dribble a basketball with their right elbow. The up and down motion of the elbow moves the bow across the string enough to produce a sound, but the feeling in the right arm is very different.

Another helpful image is to pretend that your right elbow is a marker and that you are drawing a vertical line on an imaginary wall, tracing the same vertical line over and over, down and up.

"Boil 'em Cabbage Down, Variation 2" and "Boogie Woogie" from the Mark O'Connor Method Book I, and the "doubles versions" of "Perpetual Motion" and "Etude" from Suzuki Violin Method Book I are terrific pieces to train this motion.

The feeling created in the bow arm by utilizing this vertical motion produces a rounder tone and also allows easy access to the complex accenting of the beat as developed in this book.

Pam Wiley
President of American Music System
www.americanmusicsystem.com

18. The 3-D Strum—Part 3
Chords and Harmony

See: Groove Study 20

It's our obligation as string players to figure out how to use that huge range of sound for the greater groove.

Although a groove can exist without any harmony at all, many grooves are a combination of rhythmic and harmonic elements. Non-pitched drums and percussive sounds like vertical bow strokes can define rhythmic patterns without any pitches involved, but often these solely percussive rhythms are parts of a song or larger piece of music that has notes or chords (groups of notes) incorporated from other instruments. Happily, these wooden boxes we play are capable of every shade of articulation, from the pure percussion of the vertical strokes to sustained singing tones. With great power comes great responsibility, and it's our obligation as string players to figure out how to use that huge range of sound for the greater groove.

When we add horizontal bow strokes into a percussive vertical strum, we open the door to melody and harmony. Rhythm patterns can become melodic riffs. Double stops and combinations of pitches give us the ability to play chords and imply harmony. It's time to explore some more interesting harmonic terrain.

Let's take another look at the 3-D Strum version of Practice Groove 1 that we learned in the last chapter.

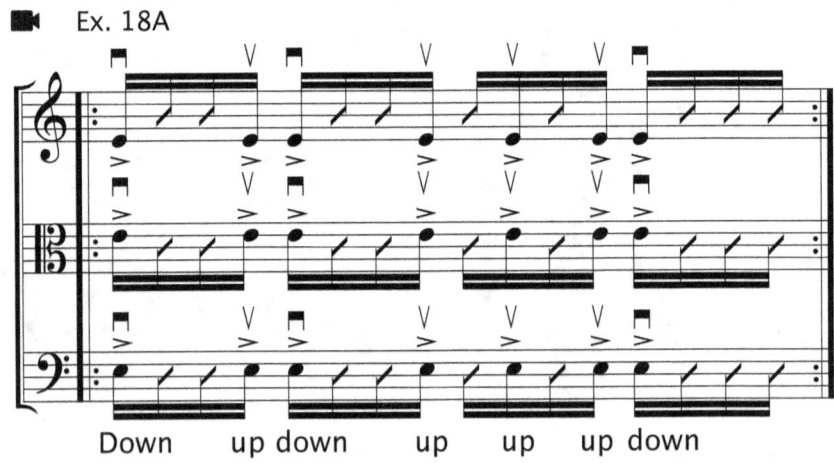

Our focus in this book has been on the bow arm, so the notes in the left hand have been mostly very simple. The 3-D groove in Ex. 18A, for instance, consists of only one pitch.

Using double stops, we can add pitches and create a sense of moving harmony. One of the easiest ways to do this is to add a melodic line to the original note—in this case, a descending melody.

Ex. 18B

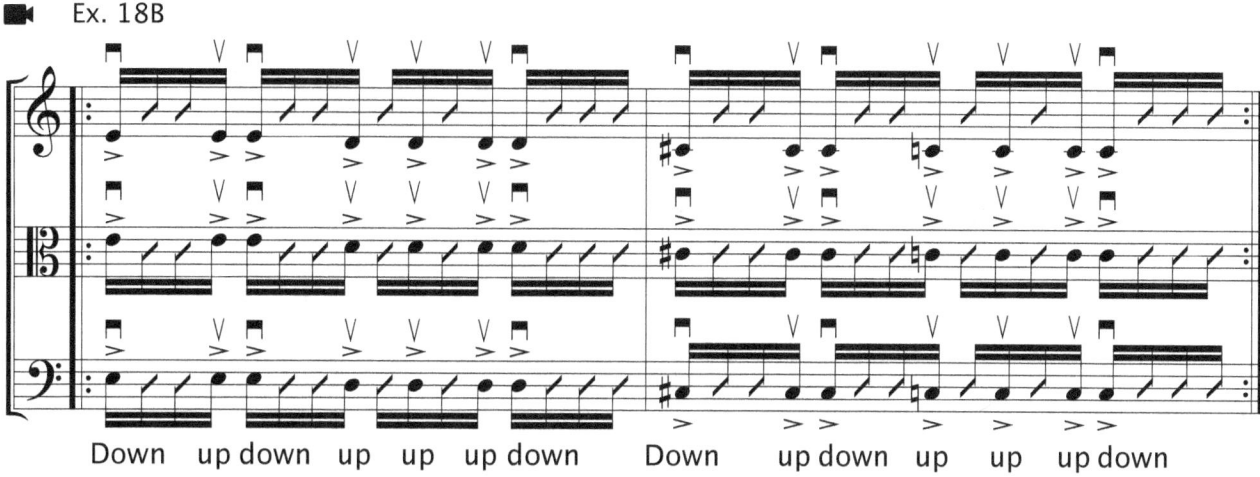

On violin and viola, it's possible to play the descending melody while also playing the repeated E. Cellos and less advanced players, play *divisi*. Bass players, stay on the E.

Ex. 18C

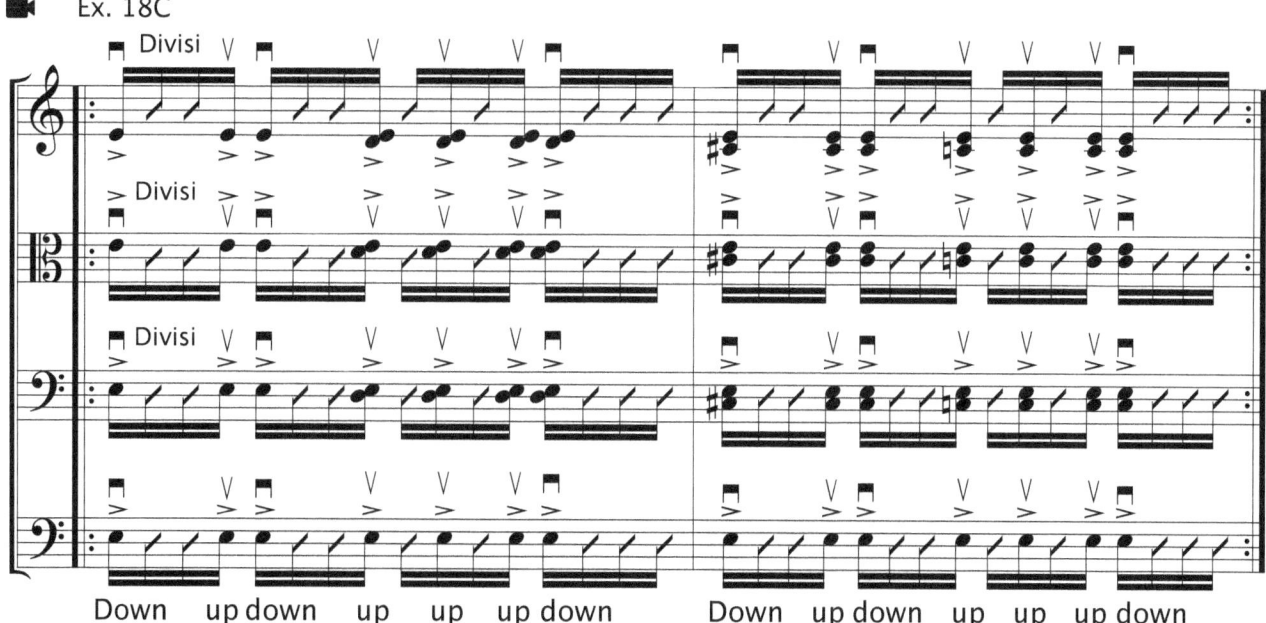

The 3-D Strum–Part 3   139

This is just one simple example of how you could create harmony. The notes could be anything at all. The possibilities are limitless. Clearly, there is a lot more that could be said about harmony and chords, but the choice of which chords to use and how to voice them is beyond the scope of this book.

As you play around with new grooves, remember that it's OK to add things to them. For instance, as we've learned in previous examples, you could easily emphasize the back beat by substituting in a hard Chop on the second and fourth beats.

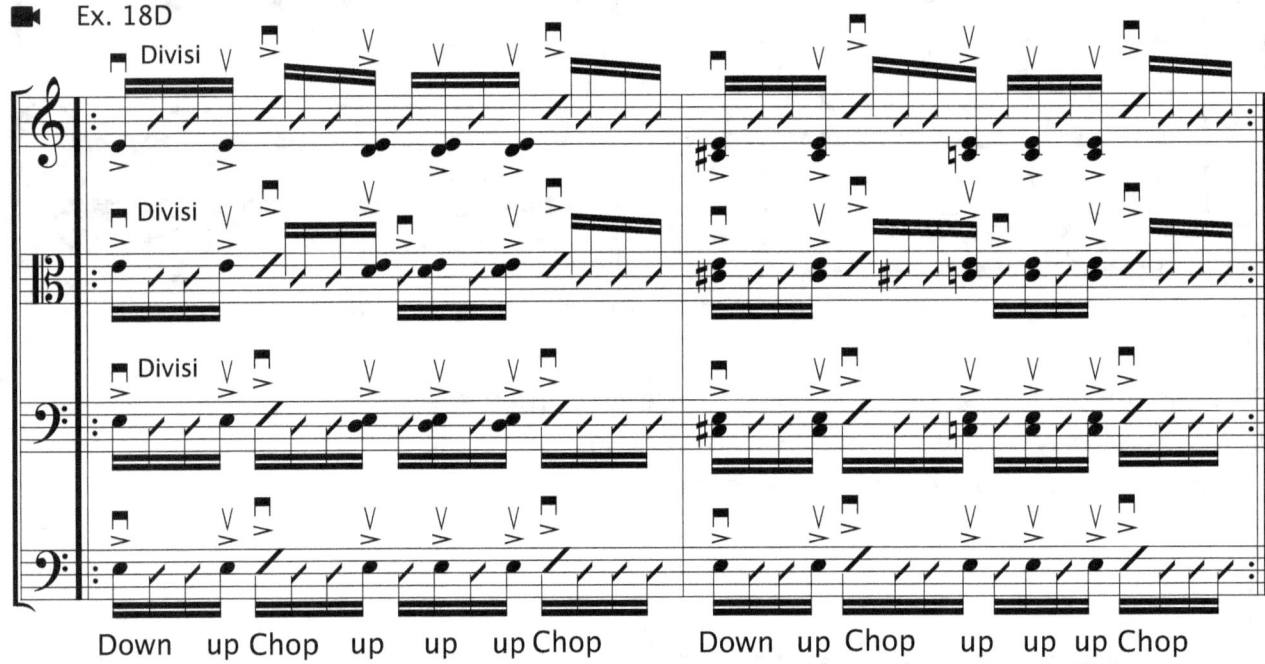

You can even double-time the backbeat.

Ex. 18E

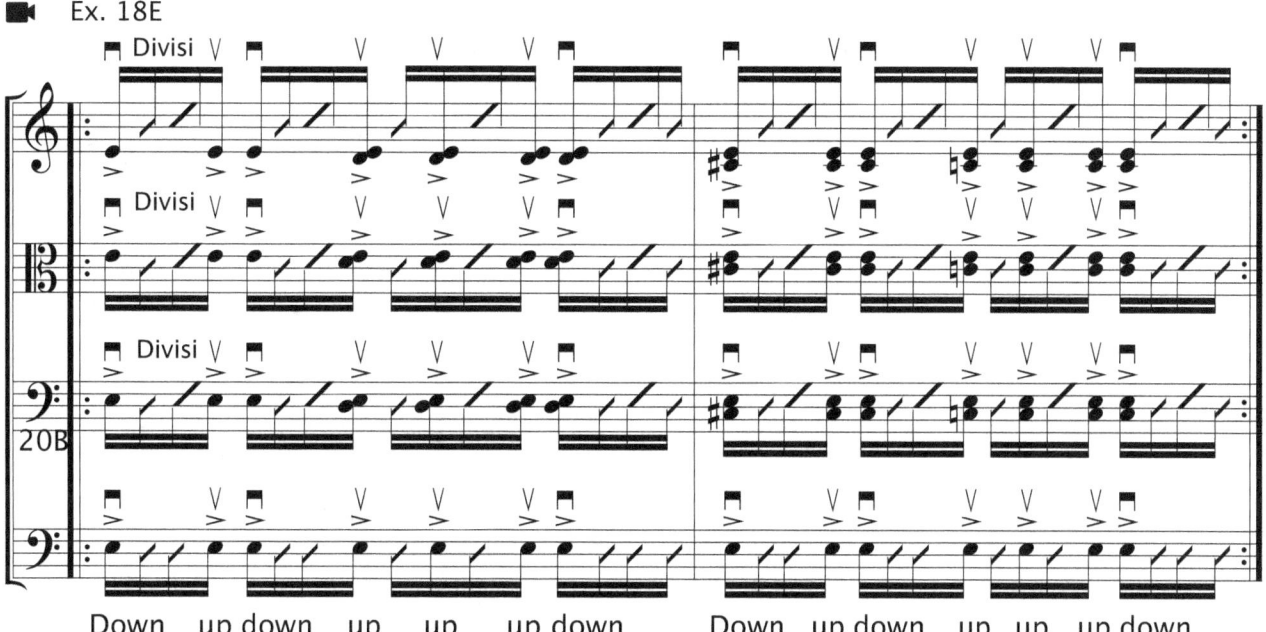

Here is the 3-D version of Practice Groove 2 that you learned in the last chapter:

Ex. 18F

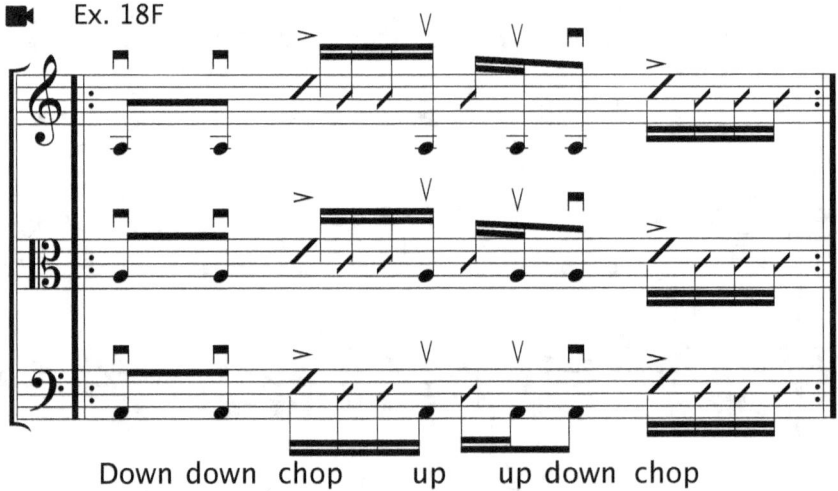

Down down chop   up   up down chop

Let's change it from the key of A to the key of D. Using only double stops, we can turn it into a two-bar progression of four chords.

Ex. 18G

Remember to stay at the frog for all the horizontal strokes.

Finding Your Way

So far in this book, I've given you the notes to play. But as newly conscripted members of the rhythm section, you may find that you are expected to play without any written music. There are many times in the non-classical world when you may be lucky to get even a chord chart. You will need to develop a simple way of finding something to play that works.

The best strategy, of course, is to use your voice. Sing along, find pitches that work and then locate those pitches on your instrument.

Find the most important pitch of the groove. This is often the root note of the key, i.e., the note D in the key of D Major. If the groove is a chord progression (several different chords in a row) the most important pitch may not sound good when sung through all the different chords, but try to find a note or two that works. You may find a harmony line, like we did in Ex. 18B.

Through intuition and trial and error, locate on your instrument the pitch or pitches that you're singing. Start out with a mostly non-pitched vertical Chop, and then start bringing in the pitch or pitches you located. Use those pitches on the accents of the groove.

That should be enough to get you started with a Strum Bowing groove of some kind. From there, it's a matter of following your ear and your imagination wherever it may lead.

The best strategy, of course, is to use your voice.

3-D GPS

Getting comfortable with a new technique like the vertical stroke is not easy, and combining horizontal strokes with vertical ones adds a whole other level of challenge. To help, here is a 3-D GPS (Groove Proficiency System) focused on putting this final 3-D step together:

1. **Vertical: Compound Chop with accents**—Start with the Compound Chop. Beatbox or vocalize the accents of the groove, and bring out those accents with vertical bow strokes.

2. **Horizontal: Find the note**—Find the main pitch of the groove. Sing it out loud, and find it on your instrument.

3. **1 + 2 = 3D**—Play the Compound Chop with Accents from Step 1, but now, when you vocalize the accents of the groove, sing the main pitch you discovered in Step 2. Change the vertical accents of the Compound Chop to horizontal strokes using the pitch you are singing.

Once you get a 3-D groove going, mess with it. Add a backbeat, or let the accents adjust themselves to what works best on a string instrument. Keep singing while you're playing. If you are having difficulty, make sure you are giving clear commands to your arm by saying the bow direction.

Once you get a 3-D groove going, mess with it.

Play
Strum Bowing Pro Tips

Now that you've accumulated the basic skills, all you need is a few thousand hours of repetition to get comfortable with it all. Here are a few Pro Tips to keep you on track:

- **If you can say it, you can play it**—for a quick fix, sometimes all you need to do is use your voice. It forces you to be specific and helps connect your brain with your arm and hands.
- **Imitate random tunes**—play along with your favorite tunes, and then choose music at random that you don't know. Try to replicate the groove of the song.
- **GPS**—If you get lost, use your GPS: Hum It, Strum It, Say It, Play It. Get it in your voice, get it in your body, get it in your brain, get it on your instrument.
- **3D GPS**—1) Compound Chop with Accents, 2) Find The Note, 3) 1 + 2 = 3D.
- **Rhythmic improvisation**—Start with non-pitched rhythms, and add a limited number of pitches as you need them. Sing what you hear in your head, and try to play what you sing.
- **Don't sit**—Stand when you practice. Get up and let your body help you.
- **Make stuff up**—Be playful and have fun. Change things around. Surprise yourself.

Make stuff up—be playful and have fun. Surprise yourself.

19. Rhythmic Improvisation
Strumming Solos

See: Groove Study 21

The beauty of the Chop and vertical bowing is that there are no pitches to worry about.

One of the wonders of rhythm playing is how it frees up the improvisational process. If you're new to creating your own musical ideas, rhythmic variation is a great way to get started. You'd be surprised how much you can do with just two or three different notes if the rhythms are interesting. The beauty of the Chop and vertical bowing is that there are no pitches to worry about. You can practically ignore your left hand! So anytime you've wandered into the deep end of the chord progression pool, you can just follow some non-pitched rhythmic Chopping back into familiar waters.

Pocket First

Anytime you've wandered into the deep end of the chord progression pool, you can just follow some non-pitched rhythmic Chopping back into familiar waters.

The key to good rhythm playing is also the key to good soloing: Jazz players say, "Pocket first!" ("Pocket" is short for "in the pocket," which is another way of saying "in the groove.") "Pocket first" means that once you get a good groove going, everything else feels right. When you physicalize and vocalize a groove, as we've practiced throughout this book, you will have naturally internalized a sense of looseness. Allow this flexibility to carry over to your mindset as well so that you learn to trust your ability to think on your feet. As long as you're in the pocket, you can get away with playing almost anything.

The Mix Area

We've approached horizontal and vertical strokes as two very different things so far, but what about the mix area in between? In the last chapter, I directed you to play the horizontal strokes of the 3-D strum at the frog, but what happens if you stray a little higher in the bow? As you get more comfortable with the idea of keeping time for yourself by strumming with your bow arm, you can start to explore the area between the horizontal strokes at the middle of the bow and the vertical ones at the frog. This in-between area can be a good place for improvising, when you may want to cross fluidly from more melodic to more rhythmic ideas. Dampened notes and percussive rhythms can be very useful when soloing. These rules are different from those of classical string playing, in which there is really no such thing as strokes that don't produce pitches.

Improv Tips

So, you're finally ready to take the plunge into improvisation! Here are my tips for those string players who have never played a note without music in front of them:

- First, do no harm. Adapted from the medical field, this means **don't disturb the groove**. Listen to what's going on around you, and try to fit in. At first, think of yourself as a percussion player. Whether you're jamming along with a recording or other musicians, use your voice, your body and all the skills you've learned throughout this book to help you find the accents of the groove, and Chop along with it.

- Don't worry about the notes yet. As you Chop along vertically with the groove, sing quietly to yourself and **try to find the important pitches that are being used.** Maybe it's the bass line, the vocal melody or an important harmony line. Or, maybe you hear new notes to add.

- As you sing along, **sneak in a few quiet horizontal strokes**, and try to match a note or two that you're singing on your instrument. If you're not sure that the pitches you're playing will sound good, employ your new skills with ghost notes and dampen the strings slightly so that only you can really hear them. It's a fine line between ghosting and the ancient art of faking. One way or another, find your way to a few pitches or short melodic riffs that sound good. This may be just a couple of notes or a several-bar phrase repeated within the ongoing Chopping of the groove.

It's a fine line between ghosting and the ancient art of faking.

Rhythmic Improvisation

Move or dance while you play. Movement keeps the beat steady, which frees up your mind to explore new ideas.

- Now that you've discovered a few notes or riffs that work, without disturbing the groove, cautiously **drift a bit higher in the bow** toward the middle. This will naturally bring you into more horizontal shuffling strokes. Now that you're more confident in them, play the notes or phrases you derived from your voice, but play them with a fuller horizontal stroke. Ghost all the placekeeper notes in between.

- Explore. Maybe you found the same pitches that you were singing. Maybe you played something that sounds even better. Or worse. This may lead you to other phrases, pitches or ideas. **Be flexible**. Follow your hunches. But be discreet—learn how to try things quietly with dampening and ghosting until you are sure of them. Venture back and forth between vertical Chops and horizontal shuffles. See what works best. Or just change it up to keep it fresh.

- Explore, yes, but rule number one is still the most important: don't disturb the groove. I encourage you to explore and invent, but this typically takes one's attention away from the steadiness of the groove, which is why it's so important to **move or dance while you play**. The inertia of movement in your body keeps the beat steady and keeps the Groovons on the grid, which frees your mind up to explore new ideas. Always keep the groove in your body and the strum in your arm. It's your lifeline.

Sing, Sing, Sing!

The more you sing and play along with your voice, the more melodic notes you'll be able to add to your rhythmic mix. If you try it every day, you'll be surprised how much further you can wander outside a simple strum or Chop pattern to add more and more melodic phrases to your groove. Eventually you will feel confident enough to jump out of the nest and fly in the clear skies of melodic improvisation.

Flexibility

It's important not to be too rigid with rules. I'm not advocating this philosophy in all areas of life, but when it comes to music, it's good to strive for flexibility—both physically and with the rules of Strum Bowing. Keep your arm, wrist and fingers loose at all times. I can't think of any circumstance when you would be better served by tension than by looseness. And feel free to experiment with the guidelines of Strum Bowing. As you practice the techniques outlined in this book, find your way toward what feels and sounds right. As you apply the concept of Strum Bowing to various pieces of music you may be working on, there may be times when Strum Bowing is helpful and times when a different bowing just works better.

What I hope to give you is the ability to hear a groove, figure out how to replicate it on a string instrument, then take that groove and be able to improvise with it and let it be a living, breathing, physical groove with all the freedom and agency to respond in the moment to its musical surroundings.

Trust your intuition, but at the same time—and this is where the rubber meets the road—really listen to what you're doing, not just what you imagine you're doing.

The only actual rule in all of this is don't disturb the groove. The groove rules. There is no rubato here, no tempo fluctuations for expressive purposes. Remember, a great groove is a metaphor for eternity—it was always there and always will be. You just ride it for a while.

I can't think of any circumstance when you would be better served by tension than by looseness.

All Notes Are Not Created Equal

TRACY SILVERMAN'S UNIFIED APPROACH to rhythmic bowing is innovative and cutting-edge, but its roots go back hundreds of years.

Baroque era violinists began playing polyphonically, creating more than one voice on their instrument simultaneously. Just as in chamber music, certain voices are more melodically dominant, and others are "filler." For example, the "cuckoo" moment from the first movement of Vivaldi's "Summer" concerto wouldn't sound as flavorful if one only played the cuckoo notes, but the cuckoo would be obscured if all of the notes were played with an equal dynamic and emphasis. Energy is maintained and the little bird pops out to the ear by "ghosting" the filler notes.

Vivaldi Summer, Mov't 1

The same concept applies when slurring, for example in the solo sections of the first movement of Vivaldi's Violin Concerto in A Minor.

Vivaldi Concerto in A minor, Mov't 1

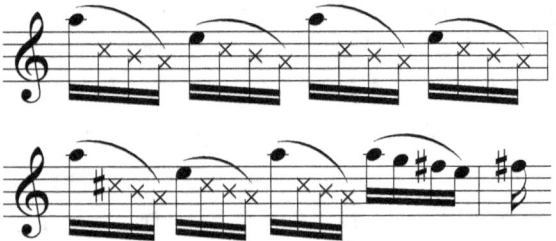

The legendary 19th Century violin virtuoso (and arguably the world's first "rock star"), Niccolò Paganini, made effective use of bowing to create a rhythmic groove. His Caprice No. 16, for instance, can only be described as funky! The variety of placement of accents within the grid, obviously serving no melodic purpose, is astonishing. Perhaps it's no coincidence that he was also a virtuoso guitarist?

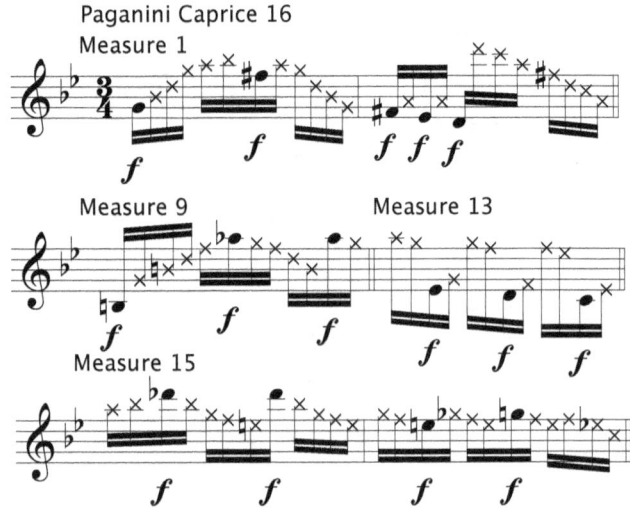

20th Century composers continued to develop and expand the tradition. The first movement of Prokofiev's Violin Concerto No. 1 uses creatively placed accents to create a jagged aggressiveness.

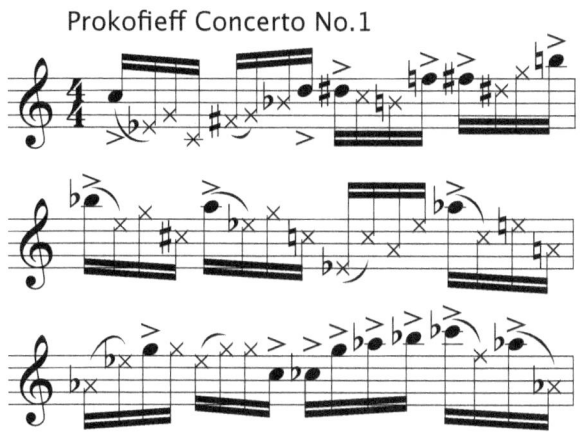

Obviously, none of these examples above contain full-fledged strum bowing, but they demonstrate how traditional classical composers have used the bow to create rhythmic and melodic complexity. In an era where classical virtuosity has focused on left hand technique, non-classical violinists like Richard Greene, Darol Anger, and Tracy Silverman have been pushing the boundaries of right hand violin technique.

Within the next generation, I expect to see classical string players' ability to play rhythmic bowing become just as normal and expected as the ability to do double stops, left-hand pizzicato, sautillé, or up-bow staccato. I also anticipate that rhythmic bowing will intrigue composers and will begin to appear in our sonata and concerto repertoire. It has begun already, with this clear indication of Strum Bowing in The Dharma at Big Sur, written for Tracy Silverman, by John Adams.

Rachel Barton Pine
Concert Violinist,
Recording Artist
rachelbartonpine.com

20. The Rhythm of Melody
Bringing Strum Bowing into Classical Playing

See: Groove Study 22

Behind nearly every melody, classical or otherwise, is an implied groove.

Strum Bowing has taught us that in order to play rhythms accurately, we need to find and honor the subdivision, a.k.a. the Groovon. This means we have to count. To be sure that our counting is steady, we physicalize the Groovon with a strum, adding ghosted placekeeper notes for rests or held notes.

This allows us to play a rhythm that is accurately lined up with an objective grid. It doesn't mean, necessarily, that this is the exact bowing we should use in performance. Using ghost notes to replace rests or held notes will change the character of the music into something that sounds more contemporary--more jazzy or funky. This is probably not what you want in a classical context. But it does allow us, at least while practicing, to experience and play rhythms—more accurately than we might with more typical slurred or as-it-comes bowing. This is important for string players to understand because the physics of playing with a bow favor balanced back and forth strokes. (See "Physics Always Wins" in "An Introduction to Strum Bowing.")

Behind nearly every melody is an implied groove.

But string instruments are primarily melodic instruments when played with a bow. When we play melodic phrases, it is often more convenient, musical and idiomatic to slur several notes on one bow and then do a similar slur on the following bow stroke. So we may have achieved a balance of longer back and forth strokes over several beats that have nothing to do with the faster underlying rhythmic pulse. This essentially cuts us off, as string players, from the sense of rhythm that is implied by most melodies. It's as if we're too busy singing a long vocal line to dance to the rhythm underneath it.

The result is that we often don't play rhythms accurately.

I believe that we can remedy that by learning how to focus on the underlying rhythm of melodies—by focusing on strumming the Groovons, Strum Bowing puts the laws of physics on the side of rhythm, rather than melody. Once we get used to hearing rhythms played correctly, we can play them more accurately after removing our placekeepers.

To illustrate this, here are several examples from the classical repertoire to demonstrate how you can use Strum Bowing to find a bowing that favors the rhythmic aspect of the melody. Violists, cellists and bassists please forgive me—these examples are treble clef only since they are intended more to illustrate a point than to practice.

It's as if we're too busy singing a long vocal line to dance to the rhythm underneath it.

Adding Placekeepers

Bach's Brandenburg Concerto #3 would look like this with as-it-comes bowing:

Ex. 20A

Let's add the placekeeper notes.

Ex. 20B

If we remove the placekeeper notes, the bowing would look like this:

Ex. 20C

Dotted Rhythms

Dotted rhythms present problems for bowed instruments because they are uneven. If we play them with as-it-comes bowing, they sound uneven because one bow stroke has to move much faster, and consequently sounds much louder, than the other.

Ex. 20D

So we often slur it as a "hooked" bowing.

Ex. 20E

There is nothing about either of the above bowings that encourages adhesion to the grid. If a dotted rhythm starts to sound like a triplet, it's because we're not feeling the subdivisions. But, we can force ourselves to feel them by strumming them and adding ghosted placekeeper notes to keep us on the grid.

Ex. 20F

Beethoven

Beethoven's 7th Symphony, often called the "Dance" Symphony, has a dotted rhythm within a 6/8 time signature. It's notorious for being played inaccurately. It often falls slightly off the grid, maybe because it's played with this bowing, the dreaded "as-it-comes" bowing:

Ex. 20G

or this bowing:

Ex. 20H

It takes a very good player to play it accurately with either bowing. It often starts to turn into something more like this rhythm, which has none of the vigor of the correct rhythm:

Ex. 20i

If it seems like I'm splitting hairs and you're thinking, "Who really cares if it's off a tiny bit? This feels more natural to me!" Well, the reason it's so significant musically is because this little inaccuracy shifts the primary pulse from two groups of three in 6/8

Ex. 20 J

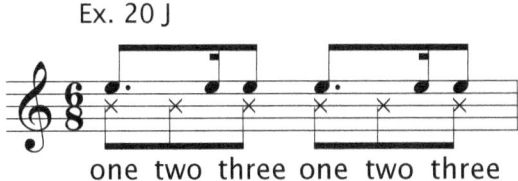

one two three one two three

The Rhythm of Melody

...to two groups of two in 2/4

Ex. 20K

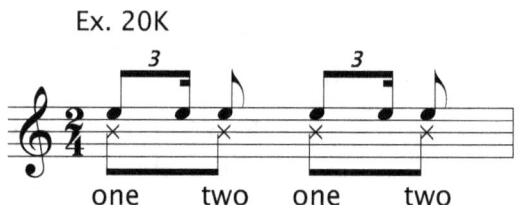

It may seem like a subtle difference, but it changes the whole underlying rhythm. Ludwig would not approve. If we go down to the Groovon level, we see that it subdivides like this:

Ex. 20L

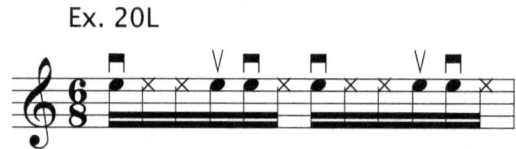

If we take away the placekeeper notes, what you end up with is this bowing:

Ex. 20M

Bowing in Real Life

It's much easier to be rhythmically accurate if you add the placekeeper notes. Of course, in most classical music, you don't get to add placekeeper notes wherever you like. But in practice, when a rhythm gets out of whack, it's a good idea to break it down to the Groovons and play those placekeepers for a minute or two just to remember what it sounds like when it lines up completely with the grid. This helps to get it in your ear so you will have a better idea of what to shoot for if you have to play it with a less rhythm-friendly bowing.

Here is the same rhythmic issue from Wagner. This is the dreaded "as-it-comes" bowing that plagues many violin sections:

Ex. 20N

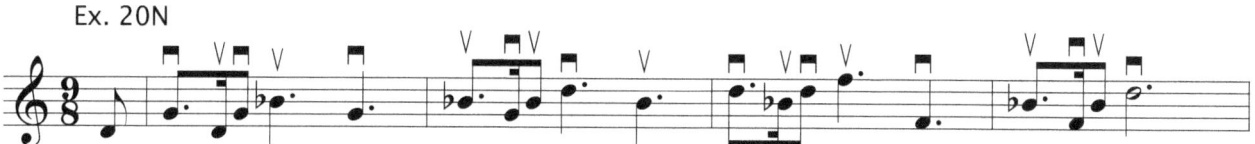

The danger is being drawn little by little into the vortex of a 3/4 rhythm simply based on the physics of using a bow so that instead of this:

Ex. 20o

It comes out like this:

Ex. 20P

The Rhythm of Melody

Please don't do this to Wagner. He can't defend himself.

Instead, break it down to the Groovon.

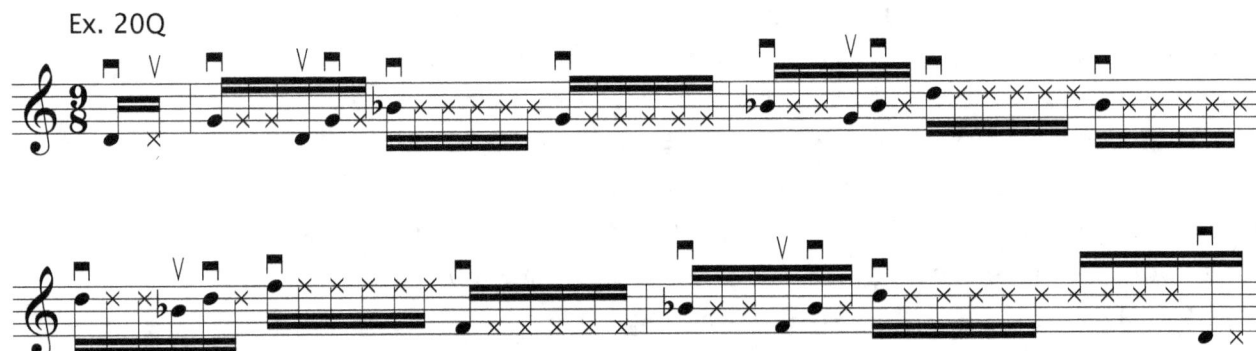

If you practice it with the ghosted placekeeper notes in order to make it rhythmically correct, you may find that it's better to retain that bowing even after removing the placekeepers, as in Ex. 20R. (I changed the last beat to an up bow for convenience.) But, even if you don't ultimately perform it that way, it may be helpful to return to this more placekeeper-friendly bowing to remind yourself of Wagner's rhythmic intentions.

The Groove in the Melody

A melody almost always implies a rhythm of its own, but if there is already a groove going on, the melody always exists within the context of that groove. The timing of that melody, the feel of whether it's ahead of, behind, or right on the beat has everything to do with the grid established by the groove.

If music is an ocean, upper string players are usually sailors, not fish. Our view is of the top surface of the sea. We play melodies, but we often have no idea what harmony and rhythm is swimming beneath us. We must return to our musical birthplace in the sea and understand that our melodies exist in a 3-dimensional rhythmic/harmonic context, not as disembodied fragments of music. Melodies do not exist in their own universes. In fact, they are often the result of a groove and a harmonic context.

Melodies do not exist in their own universes.

The melody of Bach's "Arioso" has a steady quarter note bass line going on beneath it. The bass line implies the eighth note subdivision that appears in the melody. To ignore that relationship between the pulse in the bass and the subdivision of that pulse in the melody is to miss the point, frankly.

Ex. 20S

Too often, string players see melodies like these as disembodied gifts of melodic beauty rather than understanding their rhythmic contexts, lingering over the eighth notes in a more approximate way, stretching them as an opera singer might, to bring out the beauty of the melody.

> *I certainly don't mean to discount the beauty in melody, but I'm suggesting that there is also beauty in the pulse.*

I certainly don't mean to discount the beauty in melody, but I'm suggesting that there is also beauty in the pulse and the way it moves inexorably forward—if we don't disturb it.

Free Your Bow and Your Bach Will Follow

I'm not a musicologist or a baroque music specialist, so I make no claim to period authenticity. But I am going to suggest that Bach may have intended many of his solo violin sonatas to be played with some freedoms that most classical players don't allow themselves. Let's look at his wonderful Double to the Bouree in the B minor Partita. In Ex. 20U below, the top staff is the Bouree, and the bottom staff is the Double, the movement that follows the Bouree. The double is essentially a variation of the Bouree with a double-time feel—that is, a variation emphasizing the subdivision.

In these Doubles, Bach shows us very clearly how he takes a dance tune and fills in the long notes and rests with subdivisions. On the page, each note is exactly the same size, so it's easy to conclude that Bach intended every note to be respected equally. But, is it possible that some of these Groovons are intended to be somewhat ghosted? What if Bach was physicalizing the groove and creating a steady strum, complete with ghosted notes and accents that correspond loosely to the melody of the previous dance?

Part of Bach's genius may have been designing just enough ambiguity into these steady cascades of notes that they could be interpreted in many different ways. Different accents and varying levels of ghost notes could bring out the melody one time and the dance rhythm another. The ambiguity of a steady stream of same-value notes suggests that Bach wanted the player to be creative with the rhythmic possibilities: the cross rhythms, the rhythmic rhymes and the melodic sequences.

I like to think Bach's underlying goal with the solo sonatas was simply to create something fun—enjoyable pieces that a violinist could play at home. Long before TV, radio, recordings or the internet, people filled their time at home with games, stories, literature (if they could read) and music (if they knew how to play). These well-crafted pieces are malleable enough be played over and over again with countless interpretations, providing a lifetime of fascination.

What if Bach was physicalizing the groove and creating a steady strum, complete with ghosted notes and accents?

The Pulse

There are surprisingly few instances in the classical repertoire where there is no pulse at all. Even many slow pieces like Barber's "Adagio for Strings" have a very clear pulse.

There are certainly large areas of the classical repertoire where rubato—flexibility with the tempo and groove—is stylistically correct. From Chopin to Kreisler, the manipulation of the tempo is a tool of the classical trade. But manipulation of the tempo means that there is an underlying pulse that is being pushed or pulled.

The majority of classical music has a pulse that is intended to be rock steady. Even if it only appears for a few bars, it embodies steadiness and constancy. (See Ch. 7: "The Dance of the Groove—The Power of Physicalizing.") Whether it's Bach, Mozart or Stravinsky, the stability of the pulse represents eternity and the continuity of life, so disturb it at your own peril. Because, as any doctor will tell you, without a pulse, you're pretty much dead.

Because, as any doctor will tell you, without a pulse, you're pretty much dead.

I hope this book has shed a little light on playing rhythm, and if it has not quickened your pulse, I hope it has at least made it a little steadier and made you a little more mindful of it.

For video demonstrations of the musical examples in this book, audio recordings of the 22 Groove Studies for Strings, and all things Strum Bowing related, please visit Strumbowing.com

If you have questions, thoughts or suggestions, please visit and feel free to contact me at **www.tracysilverman.com** where you can also sign up for my monthly newsletter, The Monthly Scuttlebutt.

I teach jazz and electric violin at Belmont University in Nashville, TN. For information about workshops/clinics/residencies, teacher training, video lessons or performances, you can reach me at **info@tracysilverman.com**
Visit me at:
Facebook at facebook.com/TracySilvermanMusic
Twitter: @tracysilverman
Instagram: @tracysilverman

Grooooooooove on....

Glossary

3-D Strum: A combination of horizontal and vertical strumming.

Back Beat: The second and fourth beats in a 4/4 meter.

Bowing Key: The bow directions determined by Strum Bowing; the bowing that results when you add placekeeper notes to a phrase and impose a constant down/up bowing grid, then remove the placekeepers but retain the bowing.

Chop: Also referred to as the Simple Chop; a non-pitched vertical bow stroke consisting of a down stroke and an audible up stroke.

Compound Chop: A double-time version of the Simple Chop in which the first note is stressed and the other 3 are not.

Dampen: To mute the string by touching it lightly with a finger of the left hand without producing a harmonic.

Feel: The personality that you bring to a groove; those subtle intangibles of timing and dynamics that create a rhythmic character.

Gesture Bowing: Emphasizing with your bow arm the way you might if you were speaking emphatically.

Ghost Notes: The unstressed notes in a groove; dropped notes; nearly inaudible pitched or non-pitched sounds; the opposite of accents.

GPS for Strings: A method for learning how to play new grooves with Strum Bowing. The four steps are:
1. Hum It—Get It in Your Voice: Vocalize the Groove
2. Strum It—Get It in Your Body: Find the Groovon
3. Say It—Get It in Your Brain: Discover the Bow Direction
4. Play It!—Get It on Your Instrument

Grid: A consistent framework that helps keep rhythms evenly aligned; a rhythm ruler; a.k.a. The Groovon Grid.

Groove: A consistent subdivision of the pulse defined by a pattern of accented and ghosted notes.

Groovon: The smallest particle of a rhythmic groove; the smallest usable subdivision of the beat; a Groovon is to a beat what protons and neutrons are to atoms.

Physicalize: To actualize your inner drummer, i.e. to express the subdivision physically as a strum or other motion; to allow your body to respond to a groove with movement; to dance to the groove.

Placekeeper Notes: Ghosted subdivisions that fill long notes or rests and keep you properly aligned on the grid.

Pocket: Another word for groove or feel. Drummers and bass players often refer to being in the pocket or having a great pocket.

Power Stroke: The first, heaviest stroke of the Compound Chop.

Pulse: The beat. For instance, in 4/4 time, there are four pulses per measure.

Rest Stroke: The third, unstressed stroke of the Compound Chop.

Strum Bowing: Using your bow like you're strumming a guitar.

Subdivision: 1) The act of dividing a pulse evenly into smaller increments. For instance, a quarter note can be divided into four sixteenth notes.
2) A fraction of a pulse.

Swing: The unequal subdivision of a pulse, in which the first note is typically twice as long as the second, creating a triplet. The amount of swing can vary from a subtle unevenness to a "hard" swing.

Syncopation: Accenting a normally unaccented up beat. It usually has the feeling of anticipating the following beat.